LINCOLN

AND EMANCIPATION IN THE DISTRICT OF COLUMBIA

J. C. Ladenheim

HERITAGE BOOKS
2009

HERITAGE BOOKS
AN IMPRINT OF HERITAGE BOOKS, INC.

Books, CDs, and more—Worldwide

For our listing of thousands of titles see our website
at
www.HeritageBooks.com

Published 2009 by
HERITAGE BOOKS, INC.
Publishing Division
100 Railroad Ave. #104
Westminster, Maryland 21157

Copyright © 2009 Jules C. Ladenheim

Other books by the author:

Alien Horseman: An Italian Shavetail with Custer

Custer's Thorn: The Life of Frederick W. Benteen

The Jarrett-Palmer Express of 1876: Coast to Coast in Eighty-three Hours

Abe Lincoln Afloat

International Standard Book Numbers
Paperbound: 978-0-7884-5012-9
Clothbound: 978-0-7884-8213-7

Dedicated to the 36 men lost at sea

aboard the USS *Valcour* (AVP-55) on

May 24, 1951 off the Virginia Capes.

Relieve the Watch!

CONTENTS

List of Illustrations

\

In giving freedom to the slave, we assure freedom to the free, honorable alike in what we give and what we preserve.

We shall nobly save, or meanly loose, the last best hope on earth.

Abraham Lincoln
December 1, 1862, Annual Message

PREFACE

The Emancipation Act of the District of Columbia is an early milestone in the disruptive road to liberation. Moreover, it was the first and only federal emancipation accompanied by compensation to the slave owners.[1] Although Lincoln had long desired emancipation for the District, the bill which he signed on April 16, 1862, was not entirely to his liking. Notwithstanding, he learned much from the legislative process, which guided him in his momentous decision seven months later to issue The Emancipation Proclamation.

Emancipation of the District of Columbia's enslaved involved only a small number of people, yet the black population saw in their manumission a joyful and exhilarating experience. For many years they marked its memory with a tumultuous celebration. For a variety of reasons, the District celebration was allowed to elapse, although spirited attempts are being made revive it.

This study examines the history of the District of Columbia Emancipation, charts the passage of the Emancipation Bill through the Congress and describes the evolution of Lincoln's concepts about emancipation, greatly influenced by the pressures of necessity.

I have had the privilege of using the facilities of the Library of Congress, the New York Public Library, the Schomburg Center for Research in Black Culture, and the Fairleigh Dickinson University Library. I express my thanks

---

[1] Johnston, 175.

for the courtesies shown me. The reference department of the Teaneck Public Library has been most helpful. My editor, Roxanne Carlson, has my deep gratitude for her ever-helpful efforts. To Mrs. Jean Ganley, as always, my thanks for sparing me the burden of daily chores.

INTRODUCTION

Washington, D.C., was chosen in 1790 as the site for the capital of the United States. As a condition of the compromise arrived at by Hamilton and Jefferson, relating to the assumption of State debt by the Federal Government, the capital city would be located firmly within Southern territory.[1] The presence of slavery probably played less prominent a role in the selection of the capital than might be surmised, since in most of the northern states slavery had not yet been abolished.[2]

The District of Columbia was created from flat, undulating land, ten miles by ten miles, situated at the junction of the Anacostia and Potomac Rivers, and bordered by Maryland and Virginia. Its boundaries were scouted by George Washington, acting as a legislative agent, and approved by Congress on February 27, 1801. Maryland deeded sixty-nine square miles, Virginia, thirty-one.[3]

Although Congress assumed complete jurisdiction in the District,[4] it passed only those laws about slavery as were unavoidable. The laws of Maryland were retained for the section of the District north of the Potomac and the laws of

---

[1] The Funding and Assumption Act passed during the Second Session of Congress established the capital at Philadelphia for ten years, then permanently on the banks of the Potomac (Milburn, 109).

[2] For example, final abolition in Pennsylvania (1808), Maine (1820), New York (1827), New Jersey (1846), New Hampshire (1857), etc.

[3] Lewis, 5.

[4] Milburn, 119.

Virginia south of the river.[5] In 1846 Alexandria, city and county, was retroceded to Virginia, with the loss of the 31 square miles. The trans-Potomac area had never been especially prosperous, and Alexandria wanted to rejoin Virginia,[6] so that within Washington the slavery statutes of Maryland alone were operational.

Washington grew slowly, as did its slave population, at least initially. Enslaved labor was then needed for construction. The erection of the Capitol building required the services of many dozens of black laborers, free and enslaved, who worked as much as ten hours a day for six or seven days of the week. The owner was paid five dollars a week for the services of his slave, the freed man received one dollar a day. For casting the statue of Freedom atop the dome, the skilled artisan, Philip Reid, a slave, earned $1.25 a day (for his owner).[7]

From a crude town with limited facilities, Washington began to acquire streets and a few public buildings, but early lacked the amenities of other cities. Dickens wrote of it as late as 1846: "…spacious avenues that begin in nothing and lead nowhere…."[8] An early visitor noted that "one might take a ride of several hours within the precinct without meeting a single individual to disturb one's meditations."[9]

The capitol was situated at the intersection of four great avenues, and from it led the singularly broad[10] Pennsylvania Avenue, lined with Elm.[11] It was said that "all the other streets

---

[5] Milburn, 10.
[6] Green, *Washington,* I, 173.
[7] http://uschscapitolhistoroy.usch.org.
[8] Dickens, 116.
[9] Lewis, 15.
[10] Mackay, 168.
[11] Russell, 18.

are beggared for the sake of the pet."[12] Many of the streets were unpaved, even at the time of the Civil War. There were few sidewalks,[13] although a mile long brick walk ran from the Capitol.[14] Pigs still roamed the streets, devouring garbage and swill ejected from the houses. With the arrival of the military, chickens and sheep had become scarcer. There were, however, gaslights.[15] Most water was still obtained from wells, although an aqueduct was near completion, and limited water mains had been installed.[16] Private homes were appearing in increasing numbers. Many Senators rented or bought their dwellings, while members of the House of Representatives, who had formerly banded together in rooming houses, were now bringing their families to the capital.

Most private homeowners and Washington's high society had deep attachments to the southern white establishment. The leading white families were of Virginia or Maryland stock. Of the white population, fourteen percent were born in Maryland; ten percent in Virginia and forty-one percent born in the District, but half of the last had close ties to the South.[17] Secession had greatly upset Washington society. Wrote one British journalist, "society in Washington had been almost destroyed by the loss of the southern half of the usual sojourners in the city."[18]

In years gone by, the city was "as drowsy and as grass grown as any old New England town."[19] With the onset of the

---

[12] Mackay, 169.
[13] Lewis. 24.
[14] Beveridge, II, 1202.
[15] Green, *Washington,* I, 198.
[16] Lewis, 24.
[17] Green, *Washington,* I, 231.
[18] Russell, 192.
[19] Brooks, 20.

war, it grew from 75,000 (1860)[20] to 100,000 by 1864. As hostilities wore on, soldiers poured in, a quarter million soldiers encamped on both sides of the Potomac. The streets were crowded with soldiers, and mounted sentries stood at street corners with drawn sabers, shivering in the cold and covered with mud. The interiors of the public buildings were everywhere splattered with tobacco juice, although a generous supply of spittoons had been provided. Blue uniforms of the soldiers and gold lace of the officers dominated the scene. Also seen, were paroled rebel officers wearing their side arms."[21]

Military riders galloped swiftly, splashing mud.[22] Flocks of army wagons and ambulances rumbled down the streets. Soldiers arrive "bandaged and limping, blackened with smoke and powder and drooping with weakness...groping and hobbling and faltering...."[23] As the war progressed, twenty-one hospitals were set up in churches, public halls, patent office and public buildings.[24]

Bar rooms and gaming houses were everywhere along the 230 miles of streets and seventy-seven miles of alleys.[25] Most posted signs read "Nothing [alcohol] sold to soldiers."[26] Withal, Washington was "a melancholy place" in 1861. "Nobody seemed to have faith in anybody."[27]

Gangs of blacks loitered outside Kirkwood, National and Metropolitan hotels looking for employment. The six-story

---

[20] Green, *Secret*, 33.
[21] Brooks, 24.
[22] Trollop, 325, 326.
[23] Brooks, 16.
[24] Clark-Lewis, *First Freed,* 3.
[25] Green, *Washington,* I, 250.
[26] Brooks, 16.
[27] Russell, 192.

Willard's Hotel contained "more scheming, plotting, planning heads than any building of the same size ever held in the world."[28] African-Americans were the draymen, hack men, nurses, washer men, handymen, waiters, servants, and messengers.[29] Negro vendors lined the street, hawking oysters, milk and vegetables.[30]

Slavery had been an integral part of life in the District, although only two percent of the District white population owned slaves, according to the 1860 Census. The institution of slavery was acknowledged in the Constitution, but it fastidiously avoids usage of the words "slave" or "slavery," most likely for fear of sullying that ennobling document; or perhaps because the signers hoped that the pestilence would vanish in the fullness of time. It does allude to the slave, however, in that the Constitution regarded the slave not just as property, but as something more, since for purposes of representation in the House of Representatives, the slave is reckoned as three-fifths of a white man (Article I). The little humanity reserved for the slave in the Constitution had been removed by The Dred Scott v. Sanford Decision, which held that the slave was solely property and without rights. This decision was later to prove an unexpected boon, since it facilitated, as a wartime necessity, emancipation by Presidential Edict.

Slavery was everywhere evident throughout the District of Columbia. Lines of chained slaves driven by overseers moved along the streets, past the Capitol and the Executive Mansion.[31] Before 1850, the city had one of the largest slave markets in the country, with holding pens in livery stables and

---

[28] Russell, 18.
[29] Green, *Washington,* I, 182; Hamilton, 305.
[30] Bowers, 342.
[31] Clephane, 237.

warehouses and auction houses throughout the District and in Alexandria.[32] John Randolph wrote in 1816: "...for no part...of Africa was there so infamous a slave market, as in the metropolis...of this nation, which prides itself on freedom."[33]

Some of these slaves were brought up from Alexandria or Georgetown to be worked in the city. Others, as well as many free blacks, were sheltered in shanties, wedged between stately houses or down alleys or on public land. The more fortunate of the enslaved population worked as house servants and slept in or around the house. By 1860 there were sixty-seven males for every 100 female persons of color, reflecting the departure of industry and heavy construction from the city.[34] Some slave owners lived distant from the capital. Their slaves worked in the District and surrendered their earnings to their owner, receiving, in return, a pittance, from which, in some cases, something could be saved for the later purchase of his or her freedom.[35]

Free black persons also shared a subservient and humiliating status. At the time of the Civil War, they had to register their freedom certificate within five days of their arrival in the city, and present a separate credential certified by three white men, attesting to their lawfulness.[36] A bond of fifty dollars was required of every free black older than thirteen years of age.[37] Permission had to be obtained before a meeting or party could be held in the freed man's home. Despite the free black's protests and the possession of a freedom

---

[32] Burchard, 19.
[33] Tremain, 50
[34] Johnston, 75.
[35] Clark-Lewis, 24; Hall, 46; Clephane, 250.
[36] Green, *Secret*, 47. The conditions in bygone years were even more stringent (Clephane, 230).
[37] Ibid., 181.

certificate, he or she was ever in danger of being summarily snatched up by slave catchers and carried off into slavery.[38] If lodged in jail for a suspected offence, the free black could be sold back into slavery to satisfy the fine. Five such unfortunates were returned to bondage in one year.[39] Many free men worked as day laborers, but one in ten owned property worth up to five hundred dollars. Three black physicians practiced in the city. Some free blacks lived in tenements on East Capitol Hill or in Georgetown;[40] others dwelled in shacks in alleyways. Notwithstanding the economic obstacles, a few freemen had achieved considerable financial status and owned comfortable homes. One was the proprietor of a fine hotel which catered to white visitors weary of the large hotels along Pennsylvania Avenue, with their insufferable office seekers or petitioners.[41] As in Baltimore and St. Louis, free blacks outnumbered the enslaved.[42]

Washington reacted to the Nat Turner insurrection of 1832 in Virginia by stiffening its Black Codes in response to lurid reports of two days of rampage that resulted in the death of sixty whites and two hundred blacks. Other inflammatory events which disturbed the white population included the Snow Riot of 1835 in Washington City, where a mob of immigrant white laborers damaged black homes and stores, as well as the fashionable Snow restaurant, owned by a free black; and the Great Escape of 1848, when seventy-seven slaves, some owned by prominent families, fled the city on the schooner *Pearl*, but were soon recaptured. The white establishment was astonished that "comfortably situated"

[38] Green, *Secret*, 52
[39] Item 133. "Slave and Slave Labor in DC." No date in http://memory.loc.gov
[40] Guelzo, 82
[41] Green, *Washington,* I, 185.
[42] Johnston, 76.

black slaves would choose to flee to freedom. Severe punishment was thereafter prescribed for blacks, free or enslaved, possessing abolition literature. Restrictions were made more hurtful. Blacks, free or enslaved, were forbidden to bathe in the Potomac, carry guns, patronize drinking or gambling establishments, overstay a ten p.m. curfew, and to participate in a myriad of other activities.[43] Slaves were thereafter guarded more closely to prevent escape. If awaiting transportation, they were often lodged in the District jail.[44]

The White House and Capitol grounds were convenient thoroughfares for columns of chained slaves.[45] The sight of these slave coffles offended many visitors, appalled by the paradox of slavery and a free republic. Foreigners, sickened at the plight of those in bondage, sneered at our pretensions of freedom.

Daniel O'Connell addressed some Irish-American patriots:[46]

> The temple of American freedom is there...—and slavery is there too, in its most revolting form! ...The slave trade is there—the most degrading traffic human beings is there—human flesh is bought and sold like swine in the pig market...

A Scotsman observed in 1843:

> While the orators in Congress are...proclaiming *alto voce* that all men are created equal, the auctioneer is exposing human flesh to sale.[47]

---

[43] Lewis, 43.
[44] Ibid., 47.
[45] Ibid., 44.
[46] O'Connell, Oct 11, 1843, in *Union Pamphlets* [ed. Freidel], p. 799.
[47] Hamilton, 305.

Figure 1. A slave coffle moving past the Capitol.
Courtesy of the Library of Congress.

Figure 2. A slave gang on the banks of the Potomac River. Courtesy of the Library of Congress.

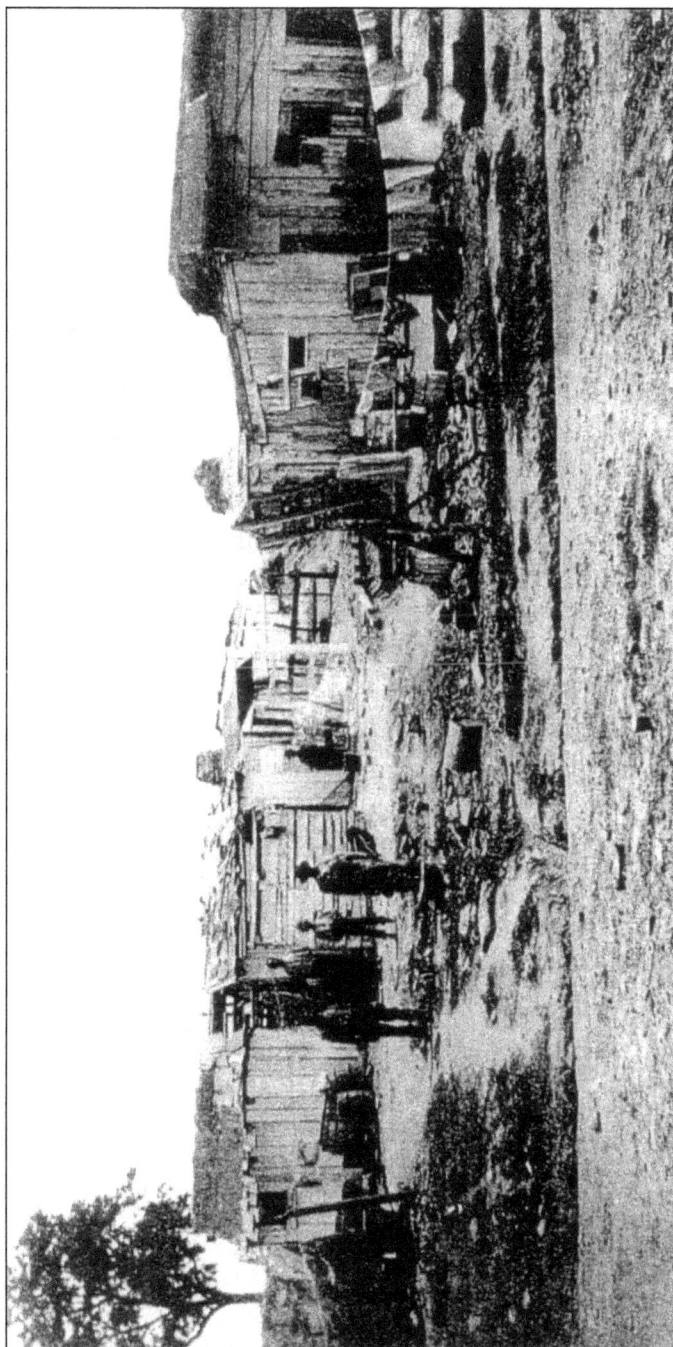

Figure 3. Free black shanties in the District of Columbia. Courtesy of the National Archives.

Abolitionists never ceased to decry the shame of slavery in the national capital. In 1828 a petition for abolition in the District was signed by 1,000 residents, some of whom were slave owners.[48] Thousands of petitions flooded Congress yearly from all sections of the country demanding emancipation for the District enslaved. Most petitions were ignored or referred to the Committee on the District of Columbia, where they vanished into oblivion.[49] In 1836, a gag rule halted the deluge of petitions to the House of Representatives. Notwithstanding, eighty thousand signatures in opposition to slavery were sent between 1837-8.[50] This interruption lasted until 1844, when, upon the repeal of the gag rule, petitions again flooded the Congress, John Quincy Adams proposed that the capitol be moved to the north, but he objected to the abolition of slavery in the District on the grounds that the action would incite bitterness in the South.[51] President Buchanan scorned the sentiment for emancipation in the District: "I believe it [the clamor] to be weak and powerless, although it is noisy."[52]

In 1850 the slave trade (not the ownership of slaves) was banned from the capital as a part of the Great Compromise. Henry Clay, its designer, believed that the elimination of slave traffic in the District "should give peace and serenity to the maintenance of slavery within the District. until it exhausts itself."[53] The slave traders responded by taking their business across the Potomac River into Alexandria.[54] Although the new law forbade the importation of slaves into the District for auction, it did not prohibit the sale of slaves held within the

---

[48] Tremain, 62.
[49] Miller, 31.
[50] Ibid., 305.
[51] Tremain, 98.
[52] Milburn, 111.
[53] Green, *Washington,* I, 179, quotes Bancroft, Frederick, *Slave Trading in the Old South,* 50-54.
[54] Finkelman, III, 323.

District.[55] Later, with the arrival of immigrant Irish laborers, the economic advantages of slavery were undercut.[56] The services of an immigrant laborer services could be purchased for $200-$300 for a year's labor; while the slave cost $1,300 (for a male laborer), and required an outlay for insurance, medical costs, shelter, food, clothing and the care for his "nonproductive" children and old people.

Nor was slavery an exclusively southern institution. There were, of course, small slave pockets in the North,[57] but, more than that, the United States must be regarded as a slave country, in which that institution, although chiefly practiced in the south, was financed by northern capital and supported northern industry. It paid for the cost of government with its import duties. Lincoln noted: "And when it is remembered how unhesitatingly we all use cotton and sugar, and share the profits of dealing in them, it may not be quite safe to say, that the South has been more responsible than the North for its continuance."[58]

From a young age, Abraham Lincoln had been repulsed by slavery. His earliest recollection in Kentucky may have been slave coffles which passed his cabin along the Louisville-Nashville Pike. In the southwest corner of Indiana, where he lived for fourteen years, he had probably glimpsed some slaves at work. Although slavery had been outlawed in Indiana and elsewhere in the Northwest Territory, the courts allowed slaves to be brought into Indiana until 1820, when the then remaining 190 slaves were supposed to be freed. More extensive encounters with slavery came during his two rafting

[55] Green, *Washington,* I, 187.
[56] Lewis, 49.
[57] For example, a handful of slaves remained in bondage in New Jersey until 1865.
[58] December 1, 1861, Message to Congress, in [Basler], V, 518.

voyages deep into slave country, along the Ohio-Mississippi and the Illinois-Mississippi Rivers in 1828 and 1831, respectively. For a half year he saw men, women and children toiling under the worst inhumane conditions.[59] Misery begets violence, and on one occasion during his first trip, he and his young companion were set upon by a gang of renegade slaves. The boys narrowly escaped, but Lincoln was left with a small scar in his neck. In later years, he glimpsed manorial slavery during visits to the home of his father-in-law in Lexington, Kentucky and was later named executor of the estate.[60]

Lincoln never ceased to regard himself as a kind of transplanted Kentuckian. His putative maternal grandfather was a southern planter. His paternal grandfather emigrated with Daniel Boone from Virginia into Kentucky, where the President was born. In southern Indiana, where he grew into manhood, the people were mainly emigrants from Kentucky and Tennessee, as were most of the early residents of Sangamon County, Illinois, his later home. He had married into a prosperous slave owning family with ten household slaves. His brothers- in- law were not only southerners, but two would later die in battle, serving in the Confederate Army.

Illinois, to be sure, was a "free" State, but the southern third of Illinois was closely bound to the southern economy, exporting, as it did, produce destined for the Mississippi and Tennessee plantations. The inhabitants of "little Egypt," as the southern third was called, was as fiercely loyal to the southern viewpoint as any resident of the deep south. This, Lincoln learned to his regret during the Lincoln-Douglas debates when

---

[59] Ladenheim, J.C. *Abe Lincoln Afloat*, Westminster, MD: Heritage Books, Inc., 2008, 27-64.

[60] Robert Todd, Lincoln's father in law, joined Henry Clay in proposing gradual emancipation to the Kentucky Constitutional Convention in 1849. (Carwardine, 24.)

he visited Jonesboro in "Little Egypt" and was threatened with bodily harm because of his anti-slavery sentiments. Nevertheless, as a transplanted Kentuckian, Lincoln believed that he had excellent insight into the southern mentality.

Lincoln was of the opinion that many southerners were at heart Union men. "It is my earnest hope that as we advance [into the South], we shall find as many friends as foes," he remarked early in his administration.[61] Only one of four southerners owned a slave. Secession had been voted in most instances, not by the southern state legislatures, but by "special" secession legislatures, which had been dominated by slave interests.[62] Trans-Appalachian people of the South were instinctively hostile to the slave squirarchy. Western Virginia lost no time in displaying its dissatisfaction with secession by withdrawing from Virginia to form the State of West Virginia.[63]

In 1837, during his service in the Illinois legislature, Lincoln offered a dissenting protest to a resolution dealing with slavery in the District of Columbia:[64]

> They [Dan Stone and Abraham Lincoln] believe that the institution of slavery is founded on both injustice and bad policy, but that the promulgation of abolition doctrine tends rather to increase than abate its evil.

> They believe that the Congress of the United States has the power under the Constitution to abolish slavery in the District of Columbia, but that the power ought not to be exercised, unless at the request of the people of the District.

---

[61] Fehrenbacher and Fehrenbacher, 9.

[62] Virginia seceded after a second round of popular election.

[63] The West Virginia Constitution specifies gradual emancipation.

[64] Nicolay and Hay, I, 140.

Lincoln took his concern about slavery in the District of Columbia with him to the 30th Congress in 1848, when he was elected to a term on the Whig ticket. On December 18, 1848 Lincoln objected to a bill repealing slavery in the District of Columbia, in that it made no provision for compensation to the slave owners.[65] A month later, after shrewd consultation with both the mayor of Washington and the leading abolitionists in Congress, Lincoln introduced his own bill for gradual emancipation. The terms would first have to be submitted to the voters of the District for approval.

The bill prohibited the importation or exportation of slaves (except those belonging to government officers). It offered emancipation, with "apprenticeship" for all children born after January 1, 1850; and offered full emancipation for any slave, provided the owner consented. The owner, in turn, would receive compensation for the full cash value of the slave.[66] By "apprenticeship" is meant that the liberated party would remain with the owner under his "direction" until he or she reached the statutory age.

The bill encountered heated opposition, and the mayor of Washington promptly withdrew his support;[67] whereupon the proposal was referred to the District of Columbia Committee and shelved.[68] Lincoln, himself, was uneasy about the reception of the bill by the voters of the District. Although he expressed confidence that if submitted to the voters, it would be supported by the people of the District, he acknowledged that if such were not the case, Congress at least would learn the voters' wishes on the subject.[69]

---

[65] Milburn, 112.
[66] *New York Times* August 13, 1862, 4.
[67] Nicolay and Hay, I, 288.
[68] Burchard, 22; Nicolay and Hay, I, 140.
[69] Tremain, 91.

Years later, as he prepared to take Presidential office, he commented: "I do not know that I would now approve of the bill, but in the main, I think that I would.[70]

It is not known whether his emancipation bill had any connection to an incident which occurred during his stay at Mrs. Spragg's boarding house in the District. Three armed men burst into the home and seized a black waiter, who was working to earn money to purchase his freedom. At the time, only sixty dollars remained to be paid. The owner, meanwhile, had changed his mind. He pocketed the money previously given him and had the slave returned to bondage.[71]

Compensated emancipation, as Lincoln had proposed, was not a novel idea. As early as 1829 the Constitutional Convention of Virginia recommended an amendment to the United States Constitution giving Congress to appropriate money for the purchase (and colonization) of slaves. Three years later a bill for gradual emancipation failed in the Virginia Assembly by one vote.[72]

Some form of compensation had been paid in many countries in which slavery had been abolished. When Great Britain abolished slavery in the West Indies in 1839, it provided 120,000,000 pounds sterling to compensate owners.[73] France emancipated in 1848 and compensated the owners the following year with ninety-seven dollars for each slave.[74] In both countries, the owners protested that the price

---

[70] Fehrenbacher and Fehrenbacher, 260, quotes James Quay Howard, "Notes on Lincoln," *Abraham Lincoln Quarterly*, 4 (1946-7), 873.

[71] Burchard, 22.

[72] Green, *Washington,* I, 141.

[73] McKim, Randolph Harrison, pamphlet published by United Confederate Veterans, Nashville Tenn., June 14, 1904, p. 25.

[74] Jennings, Lawrance, "French Reaction to British Slave Emancipation," Baton Rouge: Louisiana State University, 1988, in http//www.ohio edu/^chatain/tz/slavery/htm.

paid for the slaves was considerably less than their purchase price; and that there had been no provision made for the decline in land values after emancipation.[75] In fact, agriculture in the British and French Caribbean islands had declined drastically after compensated emancipation.

Small wonder that there was little enthusiasm during peacetime either in the North or the South for a scheme of compensated emancipation that promised little or no overt economic gain to either section; and, further, would have imposed large and very direct expense. The approximate value of the slave population was three billion dollars. Even with gradual payment and the issue of 6% bonds, the costs of servicing the bonds would have tripled the annual budget.[76] A contemporary pamphlet dramatizes the total cost of emancipation:

> It would be a beautiful sight to see, each year the blood
> and sweat and toil of the white men of the north gathered
> into a train of two thousand six hundred and fifty wagons
> [loaded with silver], *fourteen miles long*, as our tribute to
> the fell demon of abolition![77]

Some calculated the cost of the proposed compensated emancipation to be equal to the total cost of the war,[78] As a wartime compromise, its burden would be insufferable, even if spread out over forty years, superimposed on the then

---

[75] Leandro Prados de la Escosura [ed.], Stanley L. Engerman, *Exceptionalism and Industrialization,* Cambridge, Eng.: Cambridge Univ., 2004, 292.

[76] Ranson, Roger, *Conflict and Compromise,* Cambridge: Cambridge Univ. Press, 1989. in http://eh.net/encyclopedia/article/ranson.civil.war.us., p.11.

[77] Freidel, *Union Pamphlets*, 432.

[78] Ranson, 10; also http://eh.net/encyclopedia/article/ranson.civil.war.us, p. 10.

accumulated cost of the war.[79] The fact that there might be overriding advantages to compensated emancipation was easily forgotten by a nation intent on imposing its doctrines on the enemy; and by an enemy determined to resist.

Lincoln was well acquainted with the abolitionist viewpoints. His partner, William Herndon, was himself a devout abolitionist. Herndon corresponded regularly with Theodore Parker, the Massachusetts preacher, and discussed the letters with Lincoln, in great detail.

Lincoln never faltered in his desire to see slavery abolished in the District but, as time wore on, he began to appreciate the difficulties, especially with the conditions he proposed. On October 18, 1858, during the Lincoln Douglas Debate in Quincy, Lincoln expressed these reservations:

> We think the Constitution would permit us to disturb it [slavery] in the District of Columbia. Still we do not propose to do that, unless it should be done on terms which I don't suppose the nation is likely soon to agree to—the terms of making emancipation gradual and by compensating the unwilling owners.

Lincoln's dilemma is apparent. He offers a desired goal but proposes conditions which were highly unlikely to be fulfilled.

---

[79] Ranson, 13.

EARLY ADMINISTRATION

P resident-elect Lincoln tried to be non-committal about District emancipation. "Upon my word," he remarked when questioned, "I have not given the subject a thought."[1] From the onset of his administration, Lincoln was deluged with a torrent of advice about slavery. A powerful clique in Congress, led by Charles Sumner in the Senate and Thaddeus Stevens and Owen Lovejoy in the House, pleaded for prompt emancipation in the District (and elsewhere). Border State politicians and those southerners which had remained in Washington during the early days of the administration, were equally insistent about conserving slavery. They pointed out that both in the Lincoln Douglas Debates and in the Cooper Union Address, Lincoln had vehemently denied an intention to interfere with slavery within the borders of the slave states; but sought merely to halt its spread into the territories.

Regarding slavery in the District of Columbia, Lincoln's intent seems to be that of abstaining from direct Presidential intervention, and, instead, of encouraging Congress to mandate gradual emancipation with compensation, from funds provided by the federal government, subject to approval by the District voters. Accordingly, Lincoln had written to John A. Gilmer[2] of North Carolina on December 15, 1860 (before Lincoln took office) that he had no intention of interfering

---

[1] Fehrenbacher and Fehrenbacher, 7.
[2] Lincoln to Gilmer, December 15, 1860 in [Basler], IV, 151.

with slavery in the District: "I have no thought of recommending the abolition of slavery in the District of Columbia,…and if I were to make such recommendation it is quite clear that Congress would not follow it." The remark clearly reflects the fact that it was made while four of the southern states still had their legislators in the Congress and had not yet broken away to join the other seven that had already seceded following the November election. Nor was Lincoln yet aware of the tremendous abolitionist sentiment in the new 37th Congress. More likely, his statement was meant to reassure slave owners.

If the President-Elect was deferential to slavery within the states, he was adamant in his opposition to any extension of slavery into the territories. He had a long-standing belief, reinforced by his study of Hinton R. Helper's *Impending crisis,* which he had carefully annotated, that if confined to its present location, slavery would eventually expire.When a compromise crafted by Senator John Jordon Crittenden was offered, which proposed. extending the southern border of Missouri to the Pacific Ocean (proscribing slavery to the north, permitting slavery to the south), the proposal carried a codicil, prohibiting the abolition of slavery in the District of Columbia. Lincoln rejected the Crittenden Compromise on the ground that he did not want to see slavery extended into *any* territory, not even into the poorly populated territories such as Arizona and New Mexico.[3] The status of slavery in the District of Columbia probably played no part in his considerations.

At the time of his election and beyond, the prevailing dictum was that the President himself could not on his own

---

[3] The Wilmot Proviso prohibited slavery in the territories obtained from Mexico. Lincoln had voted for forty-two times for the proviso, while in Congress.

initiative interfere with slavery within the slave states. Congress and the President could exclude slavery from the territories (e.g., Northwest Territories), and could regulate slavery within the territories (Louisiana Territories); but they had no power to alter or abolish slavery within the State, except by amendment to the Constitution. The power to emancipate by Presidential edict had not yet been explored.

Shortly after his arrival in Washington, Lincoln stated in a conversation with Claude S. Morehead, a former Governor of Kentucky, that he was willing to propose a constitutional guarantee that slavery would not be molested in the District of Columbia.[4] He meant, of course, that he would be willing to make that recommendation to Congress, but of course could not be certain of its reception. Once again, Lincoln seems unaware of the aggressive abolitionist sentiment in the new Congress, which was about to convene.

He might have foreseen that considerable numbers of Republicans in Congress would insist that the time had finally come for the abolition of slavery in the District. Abolitionism in Congress had acquired a new vitality, especially since the attack on Ft. Sumter and the defection of the legislators from the last four southern states, which removed a roadblock to abolitionist aspirations. Wendell Phillips, the "notorious" abolitionist, who had previously been threatened with bodily harm if he visited the capital, could now be presented as a distinguished visitor to the new Senate by Senator Sumner.[5] Lincoln and members of the Congress attended one of three lectures given by Phillips at the Smithsonian Institute.[6] As a sign of the times, a few southern sympathizers now recognized that the sight of slaves in the District might have been overly

---

[4] Greene, *Washington,* I, 95.
[5] McPherson, *Struggle,* 82.
[6] Fleischner, 235.

inflammatory and provocative to the northerners; and that slavery could be abolished in the District, without causing lasting hurt elsewhere to the "peculiar institution."[7] Feeding the abolitionist fervor was the reception of the thrilling news that Czar Alexander II of Russia was planning to abolish slavery by Imperial Edict in March 1861.

Lincoln drew up his legislative strategy. First, he sought to encourage the Border States to legislate gradual, compensated, emancipation. Next, he wanted the *electorate* of the District of Columbia to approve a similar measure. Finally, after demonstrating that the administration intended no direct action against slavery within the states, he hoped that the southern states would rejoin the Union. In time, they too, might vote for gradual, compensated emancipation. West Virginia, in fact, did enter the Union in 1863 with a constitution providing for gradual compensated emancipation. A year later, the voters of Maryland approved a constitution abolishing slavery; but by this time, the demise of slavery in Maryland was clearly evident. The slave owners had been suppressed, and many of their slaves had fled.

Lincoln best sums up his position in a letter to Horace Greeley:[8]

> I am a little uneasy about the abolishment of slavery in
> this District, not but what I would be glad to see it
> abolished, but as to the time and manner of doing it. If
> some one or more of the border states would move fast, I
> shall greatly prefer it; but if this can not be in a reasonable
> time, I would like the bill to have three main features—
> gradual—compensation—and vote of the people—I do not
> talk to members of congress on the subject, except when

---

[7] Fish, 286.
[8] Lincoln to Greeley, March 24, 1862, in [Basler], IV, 169.

they ask me. I am not prepared to make any suggestion about confiscation...

Lincoln was sufficiently realistic to realize in 1862 that the gradual measures he proposed would not meet the enthusiastic approval of the northern abolitionists, but he believed that his policy had the best chance of enticing the seceded states back into the fold; and until 1863, he retained the belief that a rapprochement with the South was still possible.

He chose Delaware to introduce his plan for gradual, compensated emancipation. Delaware was a small border state, situated south of the Mason-Dixon Line, with a small slave population. Unfortunate for Lincoln's purposes, even small slave holdings had a disproportionately large and unshakable influence on state politics. Delaware had voted for Breckenridge, the southern Democrat, in the election of 1860, although the state had no more than 1,798 slaves (two percent of the population).

Lincoln remained in the background but chose to work with George P. Fisher, a Union anti-slavery Congressman[9] from Delaware.

He drafted two versions of his proposed emancipation bill. In the first, all slaves over thirty-five years of age would be immediately freed; all born after passage of the bill, would be free; the remainder would be freed in 1893. (Apprenticeships would be provided for minors up to the age of twenty-one and for mothers up to the age of eighteen, etc.)[10] In the other, all slaves born after passage of the bill would be free; all slaves over thirty-five years of age would be immediately freed; all others would be freed upon reaching the

[9] Elected on a Bell-Lincoln fusion ticket. Nicolay and Hay, V, 206.
[10] Lincoln to James A. McDougall, March 14, 1862, [Basler], V, 160.

age of thirty-five, until January 1893, when any remaining bondmen would be freed. Apprenticeships too would be provided, as in the first bill.

"Apprenticeship" means that minor or mother would remain in the charge of the owner and perform assigned duties. Only the name of their obligated service would be changed—from "slavery" to "apprenticeship." "On reflection," wrote Lincoln, "I like number two the better."[11]

In both bills, Delaware would be paid $23,000 a year in six percent Union bonds for thirty-one years, to be used for compensation to the owners. Lincoln estimated that the costs of emancipation would be $719,000, reckoning $400 for each slave, which amounted to half the cost of a day at war.

The proposed bill suffered an ignominious defeat in the Delaware legislature. Instead of trying to defeat the bill, its opponents used a Byzantine parliamentary maneuver. They drew up an unfavorable joint resolution incorporating in it the terms of Lincoln's proposals. The resolution was passed in the lower body by a majority and was narrowly defeated in the Senate,[12] demonstrating that the chances of passage for an emancipation bill were nil. With the defeat of the bill went Congressman Fisher's hopes for reelection.[13]

Meanwhile events were moving rapidly upsetting Lincoln's measured plans. Runaway slaves, called "contrabands," had begun to appear in the army camps and in the city: "ignorant, penniless, ragged, dirty and hungry on arrival,"[14] By the end of 1862, there were 10,000 contrabands in the District, 3,000 in Alexandria, and there was no clear policy as to what should be done with them. Should they be

---

[11] Nicolay and Hay, V, 207.
[12] Vote was 4-4, and the bill was classified as "non-concurred in."
[13] Nicolay and Hay, V, 208.
[14] Green, *Washington,* I, 276.

returned to their owners as a conciliatory gesture, under the terms of the Fugitive Slave Act of 1854 then in force? What if they were owned by rebels? Should the army feed the runaways? Put them to work? Let them provide for themselves?

At Fort Monroe on May 25, 1861, General Benjamin F. Butler designated three escaped runaways as "contrabands of war" and, heedless of the Fugitive Slave Act, refused to return them to their owners. He put them to work, but did not free them.

Representative Owen Lovejoy of Illinois made an attempt in July 1861 to settle the problem, in the form of a resolution: "that in the judgment of the House, it was no part of the duty of soldiers of the United States to capture or return fugitive slaves." The measure was passed by an 83-42 vote. The measure was merely a non-binding expression of legislative sentiment.

Further clarification for the problem came after the First Battle of Bull Run, when the First Confiscation Bill was introduced into the Senate. By the terms of this bill, the seizure of rebel property was authorized, as was the confiscation of any slaves employed in work benefiting the rebel army. Slaves captured by the Union troops from rebel encampments and runaway slaves fleeing to the Union army were both called "contrabands," and no attempt was made to differentiate. The bill passed the Senate by vote of 33-6, the House by a vote of 60-43, and was signed by the President on August 6, 1861. As modest as the bill was in its provisions, it was the first of a series of acts loosening all bonds. The act neither granted freedom to the runaway, nor did it offer aid. Both these initiatives were accomplished by later legislation. In a way, the federal government now "owned" the slave. An amendment proposing to emancipate him had been rejected,[15] thus relegating the runaway to an ambivalent status.

The First Confiscation Act was important, not because it did much for the contraband; in fact, it did little. As a new master, the federal government was morally and legally obliged to provide care for the contraband, over whom it had assumed control. In most slave localities, if a owner failed to provide for his slaves, he could be arrested and prosecuted. The First Confiscation Act assumes importance in that it led to the Second Confiscation Act eleven months later, which liberated the runaway, thus absolving the federal government from the legal (but not the moral) necessity of providing basic subsistence. Most important of all, the Second Confiscation Act lay the procedural groundwork for emancipation by Presidential edict (The Emancipation Proclamation).

Meanwhile, the field commanders were without orders or direction, concerning the contrabands.

Gen. John C. Fremont in Missouri was next to become embroiled in controversy. Not only did he not return slaves, but he issued a field order on August 30, 1861, freeing all slaves belonging to rebel masters.[16] Lincoln was incensed at the temerity of this general, who, without orders, assumed Presidential authority in dealing with the problem in a way especially vexing to Kentucky as well as Missouri, both important border states. At the time, both states were in contest. Nowhere in Missouri, except in St. Louis, was the authority of the Federal Government clearly established.

---

[15] Belz, 105.

[16] "The property...of all persons in the State of Missouri who shall take up arms against the United States...is declared to be confiscated to the public use; and their slaves, if they have any, are hereby declared freemen: [Fremont's order reprinted in Lincoln's Proclamation of May 19, 1862] in [Basler], V, 222.

When Fremont refused to rescind the order, Lincoln publicly revoked the proclamation, offering a closely reasoned explanation that Fremont's action had overreached the provisions of the (First) Confiscation Act. Lincoln expanded his reasons to a confident: "Can it be pretended that it is any longer the government of the United States...wherein a General or a President *may make permanent rules of property by proclamation?*"[17] [author's italics].[18] To Charles E. Lester, Lincoln defended his actions: "It would do no good to go ahead any faster than the country would allow...We didn't go into the war to put down slavery, but to put the flag back. No, we must wait until every means has been exhausted. This thunderbolt will keep."[19] "If Freemont needed slaves," he reasoned, "he can seize them and use them, but when the need is past, it is not for him to fix their permanent future condition."[20]

Nowhere was the contraband problem more vexing than in Washington. The senior commander of the Washington garrison was James S. Wadsworth, who, like many in the military, was ill-disposed to returning the runaways, especially to rebel sympathizers in Maryland. He indiscriminately invoked the terms of the First Confiscation Act, which conferred military protection for the contraband, without first determining whether or not the owner had been aiding the rebel cause. The civilian Federal Marshal, Ward Lamon, was a close friend and former colleague of the President, who, early in the war, had been returning slaves to Maryland, under the terms of the Fugitive Slave Act. On one occasion, Lamon's agents arrested Wadsworth's cook and lodged her in "the Blue

---

[17] Lincoln to Browning, September 22, 1861, in [Basler], V, 531.
[18] *Vide* The Emancipation Proclamation.
[19] Fehrenbacher and Fehrenbacher, 295 quotes Lester, 359.
[20] Klingaman, 75.

Jug," the Washington prison, The warden refused to release the prisoner, whereupon Wadsworth sent a squad to arrest the warden and the deputy marshal, since Lamon was then out of the city. Lincoln ordered both released and then mediated between Lamon and Wadsworth.[21]

As the contraband problem worsened, many military commanders adopted diverse practices, some still complying with the terms of the fugitive Slave Act. Congress felt obliged to indicate that the return of contrabands betrayed the purpose and spirit of the Union principles.

Unofficially, Lincoln had determined that the slaves would not be returned, not even to Maryland. To Carl Schurz he remarked: "I am engaged in putting down a great rebellion in which I can only succeed by the help of the North, which will not tolerate my returning your [Maryland's] slaves; and I cannot try experiments. You cannot have them."[22]

On December 4, 1861 a bill was introduced in the Senate by Wilson (Rep.) of Massachusetts, the redoubtable abolitionist, which supplanted the feeble House Resolution of July with a new Article of War, It provided that any army or naval personnel who delivered up escaped slaves to their masters would be punished with dismissal from the service and be ineligible for further military or naval appointment. The Senate passed the bill 29-9, the House by 83-42 and the President approved it on March 13, 1862.[23] In effect, the Act repealed the Fugitive Slave Law.

Lincoln now decided to formally lay before Congress his plan for gradual compensated emancipation. In his Annual Address to Congress[24] on December 3, 1861, Lincoln

---

[21] Lamon, 256.
[22] Fehrenbacher and Fehrenbacher, 393.
[23] Wilson, 29.
[24] [Basler], V, 35.

acknowledged the prevailing abolition spirit in Congress and proposed a constitutional amendment offering gradual, compensated emancipation "for every state wherein slavery now exists," in conjunction with a program for colonization.

The proposed amendment would, of course, require two-thirds assent by the Congress and three-fourths of the States. This was a staggering obstacle at the time. If the concurrence of three-fourths of the States was required for ratification, does the number include the seceded states? Or does it mean the states that had remained? Lincoln maintained that the southern states had never left the Union.[25]

Lincoln warned the Border States: "all indispensable means must be employed [to save the Union]. If, however, resistance continues...it is impossible to foresee all the incidents which may attend...Such as may seem indispensable, or may obviously promise great efficiency toward ending the struggle, must and will come."[26] In other words, events might compel Congress to legislate emancipation in a form less palatable to the slave interests.

As a gesture of respect, Lincoln offered to consider any other plan that Congress might propose, but for now was unwilling to adopt extreme measures. "If Congress wishes to free the Confederacy's slaves, it must take responsibility for the consequences." However, he agreed that all *indispensable* means must and should be employed.[27]

Lincoln also requested that Congress provide interim relief for the runaways and in contemplation of their eventual

---

[25] In 1865, ratification of the 13th Amendment by the southern states was made a requirement before *readmission* to the Union, and all but Mississippi complied.

[26] Nicolay and Hay V, 209.

[27] Ibid., 202.

emancipation, he asked Congress to formulate a plan for colonization "in a climate congenial to them."

The message, restrained as it was, dampened abolitionists' hopes.[28] They believed that a bolder approach was required and that public support in the north for gradual, compensated emancipation was lacking.

Another disturbing military intervention came on March 1962 when General Hunter, in command of the Department of the South, issued a proclamation emancipating 10,000 slaves in his department in Georgia, Florida and South Carolina, many of whom had been abandoned by their fleeing masters. The general may have chosen to emancipate as a way of encouraging the abandoned slave population to put in a crop and provide for themselves, since his army lacked the resources to feed them. Lincoln revoked the order,[29] asserting that when and if he himself issued the order "it shall have become a necessity indispensable to the maintenance of the government" He used the occasion to issue another dire warning to the people of the South of the consequences of rebellion: "You cannot, if you would, be blind to the signs of the times."[30] If you persist, emancipation, in one form or another, will ensue.

Runaways were choking the already burgeoning District of Columbia. They poured across the Eastern Branch Bridge and the Long Bridge into Washington or flocked to nearby Union camp grounds. "They came in pairs and again in squads, big and little, old and young, carrying all their worldly possessions, rolled up in bundles."[31] By war's end, some

---

[28] McPherson, *Struggles,* 94.
[29] May 19, 1862.
[30] Proclamation revoking General Hunter's Order, May 19, 1862.
[31] Guelzo, 85.

40,000 runaways will have descended on the District.[32] To add to the confusion, many had escaped, not from Virginia, but from Maryland, which, as a Border State, still precariously supported the Union.

Since the government furnished little assistance to the contrabands, several charitable organizations were quickly organized by the black churches and the black elite.[33] Some took newcomers into their homes.[34] Great was the need, pitiful the resources. A few kind souls were bewildered. Up until 1860 half of the District black population, free and enslaved, had considerable white blood. Now, a somewhat alien hoard was descending on the District.[35]

Not until March 1862 was the Freedmen's Relief Association established as a private white charity, to provide clothing, food and shelter for the runaways. In June, a "contraband department "was set up by the military. Military commanders registered the runaways at the contraband depot, issued passes and gave employment at forty cents a day A large contraband village was set up in Arlington, but most runaways preferred to remain in the city, closer to the action and the employment opportunities.[36] They built shacks, made from "scrap lumber, tar paper and bits of odd junk,"[37] along the Chesapeake-Ohio Canal in "Murder Bay" or on "Negro Hill" on N. 10th St., away from the "respectable" areas.[38] Some runaways were housed in an old army barrack on 12th and O Street. Their situation was difficult, often made worse

---

[32] Lewis, 58.
[33] Clark-Lewis, 13.
[34] Green, *Washington* I, 277.
[35] Ibid., 278.
[36] Ibid., 13.
[37] Ibid., 277.
[38] Klingaman, 91.

by the military, who used their services around the camps, but showed them little respect.

Meanwhile, support in Congress for the prompt abolition of slavery in the District of Columbia was rapidly growing. Congress might not be able to do much about slavery in Dixiland, thundered the northern newspapers, but it could surely act in its own backyard. The rationale for District Emancipation was incontrovertible. If freedom were to be given to the contrabands flocking into the capital, as seemed inevitable,[39] should it be denied to the District enslaved, who faithfully remained at their work?

An Emancipation Bill for the District of Columbia was introduced into the Senate on December 4, 1861. When it became apparent that Congress was going to frame its own legislation, Lincoln resolved to allow the bill to proceed without overt interference.

---

[39] The Second Confiscation Act had yet to be passed.

CONGRESSIONAL LEGISLATION

December 4, 1861.[1] A bill to emancipate slaves in the District of Columbia with compensation to the loyal slave owners for each slave was introduced into the Senate on by WILSON[2] (Rep.) of Massachusetts.

> Resolved, that all laws now in force within the District of Columbia relating to the arrest of persons as fugitives from service or labor, together with all other laws, concerning persons of color within the District of Columbia, be referred to the Committee on the District of Columbia, and that this committee be further instructed to consider the expediency of abolishing slavery in the District, with compensation to the loyal holders of slaves.

February 24, 1862.[3] Mr. WILSON introduced a bill to repeal certain laws in the District relating to the black population and moved that it be referred to the District Committee. [The bill, number S108, was referred to the District Committee.]

February 27, 1862.[4] The bill was reported out of the Committee of the District of Columbia.

---

[1] *Congressional Globe, 37th Congress, Second Session*, p. 12.
[2] Henry Wilson was born in poverty and labored as an indentured farm worker. He later served as Vice President under the Grant administration
[3] *Congressional Globe, 37th Congress, Second Session*, 917.
[4] Ibid., 962.

March 12, 1862.[5] [the House sitting as a Committee of the Whole.][6]

Mr. MORRILL (Rep.) Maine introduced an amendment that no claim be paid for any slave brought into the District after the act passed; nor paid to any disloyal owner. Also, anyone attempting to re-enslave a person freed by this act, shall be guilty of a misdemeanor and subject to 5-20 years of prison.

Mr. HOWARD (Rep.) Michigan proposed that the term "felony" be substituted for "misdemeanor." [Motion carried]

Mr. DAVIS (Opp) Kentucky moved that all persons liberated under the act be colonized out of the limits of the United States, and that $100,000 be spent for this purpose, under direction of the President of the United States.

Mr. DOOLITTLE (Rep.) Wisconsin objected to the "involuntary" colonization.

Mr. DAVIS: "He [Mr. Doolittle] will never find one slave in a hundred that will consent to be colonized when liberated...Mr. President, the loyal people of the slave States are as true to the Union as any man in the Senate Chamber…, but never, never will they submit…to have their slaves liberated and to remain domiciled among them…In ninety-nine cases out of one hundred, after they are liberated and acquire their freedom, they become lazy, indolent, thievish vagabonds…."

March 18, 1862.[7] Mr. DOOLITTLE proposed to amend Mr. Davis' amendment to make it read "with their own consent."

---

[5] *Congressional Globe, 37ᵗʰ Congress, Second Session,* 1197.
[6] All subsequent deliberations about District Emancipation were conducted by the Senate, sitting as a Committee of the Whole.
[7] *Congressional Globe, 37ᵗʰ Congress, Second Session,* 1271.

Mr. HALE (Rep.) New Hampshire spoke reverently of the justice of abolition. "This nation has an opportunity of …seeing whether…the consequences…this Senator [Davis] has predicted will follow as the result of this measure."

Mr. POMEROY (Rep.) Kansas spoke in opposition to compensation for the slave owners.

March 20, 1862.[8] Mr. WILLEY (Union) Virginia spoke in opposition to the bill. "This bill is a part of a series of measures already initiated, all looking to the same result—the universal abolition of slavery by Congress."

March 24, 1862.[9] Mr. SAULSBURY (Dem.) Delaware was uncertain of whether Congress has constitutional power to liberate slaves or to appropriate money to colonize them.

[Mr. Davis' amendment for involuntary colonization failed 19-19. Mr. Doolittle's amendment for voluntary colonization passed 23-16.]

Mr. DAVIS (Opp.) Kentucky: "You have originated in the North-east Mormonism and free love and that sort of ethereal Christianity that is preached by Parker and Emerson and by others, and all sorts of mischievous isms; but what right have you to force your isms on us? What right have you to force your opinions upon slavery or upon any other subject on an unwilling people? What right have you to force them on the people of this District?"

March 25, 1862.[10] Mr. WILSON (Rep.) Massachusetts (long speech). "This bill to give liberty to the bondman deals justly ay, generously, by the master…With generous magnanimity,

---

[8] *Congressional Globe, 37th Congress, Second Session*, 1299-1303.
[9] Ibid., 1333-1329.
[10] Ibid., 1350-1356.

the bill tenders compensation to the master out of the earnings of the toiling freemen of America...Crimes against man...have been annually perpetrated in the national capital, which should make the people of America hang their heads in shame...Here the oath of the black man affords no protection whatever to his property , to the fruits of his toil, to the personal rights of himself, his wife, his children or his race. Greedy avarice may withhold from him the fruits of his toil or clutch from him his little acquisitions; the brutal may vent upon him, his wife, his children insults, indignities, blows; the kidnapper may enter his dwelling and steal from his hearthstone his loved ones...An act of beneficence like this will be hailed and applauded by the nations..."

Mr. KENNEDY (Opp.) of Maryland (long speech) "Why not allow us to work out our own destiny and to accommodate ourselves as best we can to the disadvantages which this unhappy revolution has thrown around us?"

Mr. SAULSBURY moved to amend by inserting that anyone liberated by this act shall within 30 days be moved into the free states and distributed among the inhabitants *pro rata.* "If it is the spirit of philanthropy...that prompts you, render that philanthropy by taking...in your own midst, the slaves thus liberated...Senators, abandon now, at once and forever, your schemes of wild philanthropy and universal emancipation!"

March 26, 1862.[11] Mr. WILKINSON (Rep.) Minnesota. "It is an insult to the enlightened public sentiment of the age, that those who meet here from the free States of the Union...shall be compelled in the capital of this free Republic daily to witness the disgusting and shocking barbarities which a state

---

[11] *Congressional Globe, 37ᵗʰ Congress, Second Session,* 1357-1359.

of human slavery continuously presents to their view. It is a shame that here...the representatives of the loyal and free North...should be...hissed, as they have been in the capital of the nation and in the galleries of the Senate, by the slave-holding influences of the District."

[Vote on the Saulsbury proposition to colonize the liberated persons among the northern free states unanimously rejected, Mr. Saulsbury concurring.]

March 31, 1862.[12] Mr. SUMNER: "...this measure...is the first installment of that great debt which we all owe to an enslaved race and will be recognized in history as one of the victories of humanity"

April 1, 1862.[13] Mr. WRIGHT (Union) Indiana read Lincoln's 1848 bill, providing for gradual, compensated emancipation, subject to approval by the voters of the District. "If slavery were left alone, there would be no slavery here in ten years"

Mr. FESSENDEN (Rep.) Maine. "Gentlemen say it is a bad time to take it [the bill] up; it will be attended with injury. Whom do we injure? The slaves? The slaves will bear the injury. Do we injure the owner? What claim have the owners of slaves in the District of Columbia upon us?

Mr. WILLEY proposed an amendment to submit the bill to the legal voters of the District.

Mr.SHERMAN (Opp) Ohio. "The Constitution invests in Congress the exclusive power over this subject [emancipation in the District of Columbia], and for me, I am not willing to transfer that responsibility to the people of the District."

[Mr. Willey's amendment rejected 13-24]

---

[12] *Congressional Globe, 37th Congress, Second Session,* 1446-1451.
[13] Ibid., 1467.

Mr. POMEROY suggested that if the bill is to be submitted to the voters that it should include all the people, black and white, over the age of 21.

April 2, 1862.[14] Mr. WRIGHT read a memorial received from the Board of Aldermen of Washington, expressing "the opinion that the sentiment of a large majority of the people of this community is adverse to the unqualified abolition of slavery in this District at the present, critical juncture in our national affairs."[15]

Mr. DAVIS (Kentucky) spoke against the bill, laying the blame on the political, religious and social mischievous and noxious isms that had their origin in Massachusetts.

April 3, 1862.[16] Mr. MCDOUGALL opposed the bill.

Mr. TEN EYCK(Rep.) New Jersey suggested that the Senate wait until the Border States have acted on the President's proposal. "If Maryland and Delaware should vote to abolish slavery according to the plan proposed by the President…slavery in this district would speedily die out of itself."

---

[14] *Congressional Globe, 37th Congress, Second Session,* 1473-1479.
[15] Appendix, *Ibid*, 32 Council # 59
    "Board of Aldermen
    Joint Resolution of Instruction
Be it resolved by the Board of Aldermen, Board of Common Counsel of the City of Washington, that the counsels…deem it not impertinent respectfully to express the opinion that the sentiment of a large majority of the people of this community is adverse to the unqualified abolition of slavery in this district and the present critical juncture in our national affairs and be it further resolved…to urge…so shaping any legislation…as to provide just and proper safeguards against converting this city…into an asylum for free negroes, a population undesirable in every American community"(Berlin, 37).
[16] *Congressional Globe, 37th Congress, Second Session,* 1515-1520.

Mr. SUMNER moved to amend by allowing blacks to testify in their own behalf before the proposed emancipation commission. [Amendment passed 26-20]

Mr. WRIGHT proposed gradual emancipation. [Amendment failed 10-27]

Mr. CLARK (Rep.) New Hampshire proposed that the owner must not have borne arms against the United States. [Amendment adopted]

Mr. BROWNING proposed that the sum paid for an enslaved person be increased from $ 300 to $ 500 and that half be given to the liberated slave upon evidence that he has settled outside the United States. [Motion rejected]

Mr. COLLAMER (Rep.) Vermont moved to add that slave owners file with the Circuit Court of the District lists of their slaves; and that the clerk give all freed persons a certificate.[Sustained 27-10]

Mr. POMEROY. Mr. Pomeroy argued that the proposed bill was unconstitutional since the original Maryland slave law, upon which the laws of the District are based, enslaved for only two generations—during the life of the slave (*durante vita*) and his children.

Mr. DOOLITTLE offered up his amendment for voluntary colonization. [Sustained 27-10]

Mr. POWELL. "I regard this bill as unconstitutional, impolitic, unjust to the people of the District of Columbia...The bill is unjust...because it deprives them of one of their domestic institutions...You do not give them a fourth of the value of their property...every one in the Senate knows that many of those negroes are worth three or four times that amount..."

Mr. BAYARD (Dem.) Delaware. "The effect of this bill, in my judgment, will be deleterious."

[The bill was put to a vote and passed yeas 29, nays 14. The bill was then sent to the House of Representatives]

HOUSE OF REPRESENTATIVES

April 10, 1863.[1] [sitting as Committee of the Whole][2]

Mr. STEVENS (Rep.) Pennsylvania introduced Bill # S 108, entitled "An act for the release of certain persons held to service or labor in the District of Columbia," etc.

Mr. WEBSTER (Union) Maryland moved to table. [Laughter. Motion failed]

Mr. THOMAS (Rep.) Massachusetts) "I desire the extinction of slavery with my whole mind and heart...I watch the working of events with devout gratitude and patience."

April ll, 1862.[3] Mr. STEVENS moved that the debate be closed in one hour.

Mr. Colfax amended the motion to lengthen the discussion to two hours. [Motion carried]

Mr. NIXON (Rep.) New Jersey (long speech) stated that he preferred gradual emancipation, but if immediate emancipation with compensation is the sentiment of the House, he was prepared "to vote to remove forever the blot of slavery from the national capital."

Mr. BLAIR (Rep) Missouri (long speech) praised the President for his policy which "commends itself to the lovers of the Union and of freedom.

---

[1] *Congressional Globe, 37th Congress, Second Session,* 1614-1620.

[2] All subsequent deliberations on District Emancipation were conducted by the House, sitting as a Committee of the whole.

[3] *Congressional Globe, 37th Congress, Second Session,* 1629-1648.

Mr. CRITTENDEN (Union) Kentucky opposes the bill "You may produce much mischief by this measure. What is the good? Slavery has been, under one influence or another, disappearing from this district for years…Let slavery alone. It will go out like a candle."

Mr. BINGHAM of Ohio "Slavery is a hideous anachronism coming to us out of the barbarian and dead of night of the past, with no good in it, bringing no good with it, and allied to no good about it… Those who oppose this bill…reiterate the old dogma of tyrants, that the people are made to be governed, and not to govern…I would pass this bill for…giving a new assurance that the Republic still lives and gives promise not to disappoint the hopes of the struggling natives of the earth."

Mr. RIDDLE (Rep.) of Ohio spoke warmly for the bill.

Mr. ROLLINS (Rep.) New Hampshire. "The abolition of slavery in the District of Columbia is…a deed of justice and mercy that this people cannot omit to perform. Justice demands that the arch enemy of our government and instigator of all our present calamity, who still lurks in the chosen centre of the Republic…shall be expelled…Mercy…demands for the victims of this too-long-endured oppression their restoration to the primal rights of humanity."

Mr. BLAKE (Rep.) Ohio "…it [the bill] will elevate us in the eyes of all civilized nations…"

Mr. VAN HORN (Rep.) New York. "Every line and every syllable [of the bill] is pregnant with a just and true sentiment."

Mr. ASHLEY (Rep.) Ohio "The golden morn so anxiously looked for by the friends of freedom in the United States has dawned. A second national jubilee will henceforth be added to the calendar…"

Mr. HUTCHINS (Rep.) Ohio "This bill will make the national capital *free;* and then the statue of Liberty [atop the capitol[4]] ...will be a fitting ornament on the finished dome..."

Mr. STEVENS moved to close the debate.[Motion failed 56-73]

Mr. RICHARDSON (Dem.) Illinois moved to allow one more hour.[Motion passed]

Mr. WRIGHT (Dem.) of Pennsylvania moved to amend the bill so that it would not go into operation unless approved by majority of the citizens of the District.[Amendment failed]

Mr. TRAIN (Rep.) Massachusetts proposed an amendment that if any slave owner is dissatisfied by the decision of the emancipation commission concerning compensation, he may within three months, appeal to the District Court for a jury trial.[Amendment failed 53-65]

Mr. HARDING (Opp.) of Kentucky proposed an amendment removing the limit of the appraisal sum of $300, an amount which he said would rob the owner.

Mr. LOVEJOY (Rep.) Illinois opposed the amendment. "Every slave here has been robbed and stolen, and every man who holds a slave is a man-thief."

Mr. WICKLIFFE (Opp.) Kentucky opposes allowing slaves to testify against their masters before the commission.

Mr. STEVENS (Rep.) Pennsylvania "I trust that this committee will not so far continue an outrage as not to allow any man of credit, whether he be black or white, to be a witness. [Wickliffe amendment rejected]

Mr. VALLANDIGHAM (Opp.) Ohio "There were not ten men in the Thirty-sixth Congress of the United States who would have recorded their votes in favor of the abolition of slavery in the District of Columbia...We have this bill brought

---

[4] The unfinished statue of Freedom by Thomas Crawford was then being cast by enslaved foundry workers.

forward as the beginning of a grand scheme of emancipation; and there is no calculation where that scheme is to end."

Mr. MENZIES (Union) Kentucky moved to amend so that children born are to be free after May 1 and any slave brought into the District would be free [Amendment failed]

[The Committee of the Whole dissolved, and Mr. Dawes reported the bill to the House, without amendment]

Bill # S 108 passed the House of Representatives 92-38.

The final bill[5] has the following features: slavery in the District would cease; a commission would be appointed by the President and confirmed by the Senate which would review claims and apportion value of slaves, the per capita average not to exceed $ 300; the slave owner to present to the commission a certificate of the value of the slave and would pay a fee of fifty cents; the commission could summon witnesses, and receive compensation for their labor; one million dollars to be assigned the commission for payment of claims; each owner to furnish a detailed record of his slave holdings to the commission, who would issue a certificate of freedom to each slave. at a cost of twenty-five cents; punishment to be prescribed for kidnapping of District slaves; one hundred thousand dollars to be appropriated for colonization in Hayti (!) or Liberia or any other country "as the President may determine"[6] Also, as a corollary to colonization, provision to be made for special and specific benefits to be given the liberated slave for relocation.[7]

---

[5] Appendix A.
[6] Quarles, 109.
[7] Belz, 108.

EMANCIPATION SUPPLIMENTAL BILL

SENATE

June 12, 1862.[1] Mr. WILSON (Rep.) Massachusetts introduced a bill (S-351) supplemental to the District of Columbia Emancipation Act, approved April 16, 1862. The bill was read twice and referred to the Committee on the District of Columbia.

June 24, 1862.[2] Mr. GRIMES (Rep.) Iowa, Chairman of the District committee reported the bill back with amendments.

July 7, 1862.[3] Mr. GRIMES explained the bill. Te first section preserved the rights of infants, minors, absent officers of the armed forces, unmarried women, mentally impaired and others, and allows their guardians or agents to present claims in their behalf. The second section frees all slaves owned by residents of the District of Columbia, regardless of where the slave resides. The third section frees all slaves employed in the District of Columbia on or after April 16, 1862, although the owner may reside elsewhere. A fourth section authorizes the appointment of a solicitor by the committee.

Mr. SUMNER (Rep.) Massachusetts offered an amendment that in all judicial proceedings in the District of Columbia, no witness henceforth would be excluded because of color. [Amendment passed 25- 11]

[The Supplemental Act was passed 29-6]

---

[1] *Congressional Globe, 37ᵗʰ Congress, Second Session,* 2671.
[2] Ibid., 2892.
[3] Ibid., 3136-3138.

HOUSE OF REPRESENTATIVES

July 9, 1862.[4] Mr. ASHLEY (Rep.) of Ohio introduced the supplemental bill.

Mr. CALVERT (Opp.) Maryland moved to strike out the fourth section of the bill, which he claimed interferes with the rights of the slaveholders. [Motion defeated]

Mr. WICKLIFFE (Opp) of Kentucky "As I understand the reading…if a man…in Maryland sends his Negro…into the city [D.C.]…he [the slave] is set free"

Mr. COX (Dem.) Ohio moved to table the bill.[Motion defeated 28-69]

Mr. RICHARDSON (Dem.) Illinois moved to adjourn [motion defeated 28-69]

Mr. PENDLETON demanded a vote on the bill.

[Bill passed 69-36]

[The Bill was sent to the President, who approved and signed it on July 12, 1862 [12 Stat. 538].

---

[4] *Congressional Globe, 37th Congress, Second Session,* 3215-3216.

THE PRESIDENT DELIBERATES

The passage of the bill by Congress drew a full range of newspaper comments. The *National Intelligencer* of April 12 noted that few people would regret the demise of slavery in the District, since slavery was undergoing gradual extinction, but "this sudden emancipation disturbs the [white] population and alarms the border states."[1] On the other hand, some southern sympathizers concluded that abolition in the District might appease the national antipathy towards slavery without molesting States Rights.[2] The *National Republican* supported the bill, noting that the city would benefit "from the free principles and free industry." The *Star* believed that the average sum of $300 paid for the slave was vastly insufficient.[3]

Throughout Congressional deliberations, Lincoln held firm to his beliefs in compensation and colonization; and through his clandestine supporters in Congress, he insured that these measures would be incorporated into the bill. His long-cherished hope that the bill would be submitted to the voters in the district was dispelled when the petition presented by the Board of Aldermen was received[4] and by the loud and frequent outbursts of disapproval of the bill coming from the galleries during the debates.[5] Congress knew better than to

---

[1] Tremain, 93.
[2] Fish, 286.
[3] Green, *Secret City*, 60.
[4] *Congressional Globe, 37th Congress, 2nd Session*, 1476.
[5] Ibid., 1357.

entrust the welfare of the chickens to the benevolence of the fox.

The bill cleared the Congress on April 11[6] but, unaccountably, sat in limbo until April 13, when it was brought to the President by Senator Orville H. Browning. It lay on Lincoln's desk for three days. In its final version, the bill substitutes such the niceties of phrases like "persons held to service or labor," for "slaves" and "involuntary servitude," for "slavery."[7]

Many speculated that the President would not sign the bill. There is an apocryphal and oft-repeated story told by Orville H. Browning that Charles Wickliffe, a Kentuckian, was in Washington, accompanied by two sickly slaves. He asked Lincoln to give him time to depart the city with his slaves, who "would not be benefited by freedom."[8] This implies that Lincoln was from the beginning ready to sign the bill and delayed merely to oblige a friend. Such was clearly not the case.

While Lincoln procrastinated, Senator Sumner twittered him. "Do you know who at this moment is the largest slave holder in the United States? It is Abraham Lincoln, for he holds all the 3,000 slaves of the District of Columbia"[9] "The bill...seems to sleep the sleep that knows no waking," wrote Frederick Douglass[10] "How slow this child of freedom is being born," he wrote. "The wait is difficult to endure." He tried to understand Lincoln: "Carrying on the revolution in America very slowly, that he may make emancipation sure...certainly if the Lord wanted slow work to be done, He

---

[6] April 12 was the anniversary of the attack on Fort Sumter.

[7] Clark-Lewis, 98; Except in section 3, where the word "slave" crept in.

[8] Fehrenbacker and Fehrenbacker, 64 (quotes Browning I, 541).

[9] Sandburg, I, 577.

[10] Douglass' Monthly, March 1863, quoted in Foner, *Life & Writings of Frederick Douglass,* III, 231.

could not have employed a better hand than Old Abe."[11] Henry Ward Beecher asked subtly if he was going to sign the bill before the *Independent* went to press. Lincoln did not reply.[12] On April 11, the Bishop Daniel Payne of the black M.E. Church also asked if he will sign. Lincoln did not answer.[13] Meanwhile, some slave owners in nearby Maryland and Virginia took advantage of the delay by sending their slaves further south.[14]

Still Lincoln procrastinated. The bill would not be submitted to the voters; manumission was immediate, not gradual. All true, but if he vetoed the bill and sent it back for revision, Congress had the votes to override his veto.[15] Were they to do so, Lincoln would loose his reins of leadership.

All kinds of speculations were making the rounds. Some claimed that it was Lincoln who had prompted the unfavorable editorials about District emancipation which had appeared in the *National Intelligencer*. The *Journal of Commerce* reported that Lincoln was determined to veto.[16]

On April 7, 1862, in hopeful anticipation of the passage of the bill, the House of Representatives had appointed nine members to scout for possible locations for colonization.

Colonization was an old chestnut which had been roasting in the fire for four decades. It had been offered frequently to newly manumitted African Americans (never to the enslaved), in accordance with the precept that the free black person would be better off away from the United States:

---

[11] *Douglass' Monthly*, March 1863, quoted in Foner, *Life & Writings of Frederick Douglass,* II, 143.
[12] Quarles, 104.
[13] Ibid.
[14] Goodwin, 460.
[15] Quarles, 104.
[16] *New York Times*, April 12, 1862, 4.

"This country belongs to the white man and not to the negro, and that, in our is the purist philanthropy, and seeks to place upon the shores of Africa again, those whom cupidity as stolen from their native soil."[17]

Many of the enthusiastic supporters of colonization had been white southerners. Jefferson was an early supporter, as was Henry Clay, Lincoln's *beau ideal*. Over the years, several states had contributed to the costs of resettlement, including New Jersey, Pennsylvania, Missouri and Maryland. On June 26, 1857 Lincoln had said in his speech at Springfield: "Let us be brought to believe it is morally right…to transfer the African to his native clime, and we shall find a way to do so, however great the task may be."[18]

Congress designated a former agent of the American Colonization Society as "Commissioner of Emigration" to consider, among other places, the Danish West Indies, Dutch Guinea, British Guinea, British Honduras, Guadeloupe and Equator.[19]

Liberia had long been a favorite destination for colonization. Harriet Beecher Stowe sent George and Eliza Harris to Liberia as a happy ending to *Uncle Tom's Cabin.* Lincoln could not know that the forbears of most American blacks came not from Liberia or thereabouts but from the Niger Valley and Niger Delta.[20]

Liberia had first begun to be colonized in 1821, under the aegis of the American Colonization Society, when a party of twenty-two black emigrants settled on a small island, later called Monrovia, after President Monroe. The project was

---

[17] A Pennsylvania newspaper is quoted in http://www.slavenorth.com/colonize.htm.
[18] [Basler], II, 398
[19] Staudenraus, 246.
[20] Blanchard, 32.

sponsored by the ACS for a variety of reasons: an evangelical desire to spread the Christian faith, an effort to return the black Diaspora to its homeland, and, less charitably, as a ploy to deny the Negro his just rights and opportunities in the United States. Between 1820-40, 4,000 African-Americans had settled in Liberia; 13,000 by the end of the 1860's.[21] The Republic of Liberia had been established in 1847, but prior to the 37th Congress, the country had been accorded no formal diplomatic recognition[22] from the Southern- dominated Congress, which abhorred the thought of receiving a black minister clad in ceremonial diplomatic attire. Liberia's credentials were finally recognized when two months after official recognition of Liberia in June 1862, Joseph Roberts, the ex-President of Liberia, visited Washington and was well received. As slight as the matters may have seemed to some, according the long-delayed recognition gave great satisfaction to the abolitionist legislators.

Lincoln had some slight personal experience with Liberia colonization. He was once approached to represent a slave holder who owned property in Kentucky and Illinois. It was the owner's practice to take his slaves into Illinois in the spring and return them to Kentucky after harvest, a practice not unknown. He had a slave woman who was married to his Illinois overseer. After living two years in Illinois, she had a disagreement with the overseer, and the owner threatened to send her back to Kentucky. Lincoln eventually declined to represent the owner. The case was heard in the Illinois courts and the woman was freed. She and her husband then decided to emigrate to Liberia. Lincoln's partner, William Herndon, contributed to the expenses. Later, a Baptist minister visited the couple in Liberia and was told that they had been scorned

---

[21] Appish and Gates, I, 187.
[22] Finkelman, II, 273.

and cheated by the Liberians and were now living in appalling conditions.[23]

Haiti was another favorite destination. Hispaniola had been early settled by the Spanish, but the French acquired the western third and named it Saint Domingue. A half million slaves tilled crops of coffee, cotton, sugar cane and indigo and made Haiti the richest colony in the West Indies. In 1791, with the onset of the French Revolution, insurrections began in that country and lasted until 1804. Among the leaders of the revolt was Toussaint L'Ouverture. After the abolition of slavery in 1796, Toussaint changed sides and fought with the French, becoming in time a general-in-chief, who ruled Haiti, although nominally under French sovereignty. In 1802 France invaded Haiti and in four months overran the island. Toussaint was imprisoned in the interior and later died in captivity. When the French withdrew, the island became independent, with a succession of black rulers, which resonated pleasantly with many African-Americans.[24]

An attempt had been made to settle 450 black emigrants on Cow's Island (Ile a Vache) off the coast of Haiti. Lincoln, himself, signed the contract with the promoter a day before he issued the Emancipation Proclamation.[25] Later, one hundred settlers died of smallpox; the remainder had to be evacuated back to the States.[26]

Lincoln's barber, William de Fleurville, ("Billy") was born in Haiti. Lincoln first met him in New Salem and had lent him money. He later moved to Springfield and began the first

---

[23] Blanchard, 31.
[24] Finkelman, III, 243.
[25] Staudenraus, 249; Neely, 63.
[26] Blanchard, 32.

barber shop in the city,[27] with Lincoln as "Uncle Billy's" favorite customer.

Lincoln made his woefully simplistic feelings about colonization known to a group of visiting Negro dignitaries on August 14, 1862. "I do not know how much attachment you may have toward our race. It does not strike me that you have the greatest reason to love them. But still you are attached to them, at all events. "If I could get 25 [to start a colony], it would make a start."[28]

He was shocked to learn that these men considered themselves just as American as the white man, and that they had no intention of willingly leaving the United States, on whose shores their people had first arrived a year before the Pilgrims. Frederick Douglass, like many other African-Americans, was succinct in his criticism of colonization. He wrote in 1849[29]: "We are of the opinion that the free colored people generally mean to live in America—not in Africa...Here we are and here we will remain." The *Evening Star* summed up the universal black sentiment about colonization on April 30' 1862: "The American Negro is quite different from the African or Haytian Negro...We are colored Americans and we want a home on American soil." Garrison sums it up in the *Liberator*: "Can anything be more puerile, absurd, illogical, impertinent and untimely?"[30]

Notwithstanding, Lincoln refused to abandon completely his views on colonization, reinforced toward the end of the war by concerns about armed Negro soldiers returning to the hostile south and waging guerilla battle.[31]

[27] Blanchard, 119.
[28] August 14, 1862, Lincoln to a Negro Deputation, in [Basler], V, 370.
[29] Foner, *Frederick Douglass,* III, 260.
[30] Foner, Eric, *Our Lincoln,* 183.
[31] Fehrenbacher and Fehrenbacher, 73; quotes Rice, A.T., *Reminiscences of Abraham Lincoln,* 150.

Lincoln signed the DC Emancipation Bill on April 16, 1862 and sent the Act[32] back to Congress at 1 pm. "Little did I dream in 1849 when I proposed to abolish slavery in this capital and could scarcely get a hearing ...that it will be so soon accomplished," he remarked. Although not completely satisfied with the bill, he could have vetoed it and asked for revisions, but in the end decided to accept it. He wrote to the Congress:

> The Act entitled 'An Act for the release of certain persons held to service or labor in the District of Columbia' has this day been approved and signed.
>
> I have never doubted the constitutional authority of congress to abolish slavery in this District; and I have ever desired to see the national capital feed from the institution in some satisfactory way Hence there has never been in my mind any question upon the subject, except the one of expediency...

He added:

> If there be matters within and about this act, which might have taken a course or shape, more satisfactory to my judgment, I do not specify them. I am grateful that the two principles of compensation and colonization are both recognized and practically applied in the act.

With shrewd, almost pettifogging legal insight, he suggested to Congress a way to strengthen the bill's legitimacy:

> It is startling to say that Congress can free a slave within a state...and yet if it were said that ownership of the slave

---

[32] 12 Statute, 376.

had first been transferred to the nation, and that Congress had liberated him, the difficulty would at once vanish.[33]

Such was the sham followed during the emancipation process. The ownership of the slave was first transferred to the United States as an article of "property" (First Confiscation Act), and the bondman was then liberated by Congress and the President (Second Confiscation Act) or by the President (Emancipation Proclamation), although in the later instance the intermediate transfer step had been omitted.

Lincoln was somewhat disappointed in the bill. "It should have been for gradual emancipation," he told Senator Browning. "Now families would at once be deprived of cooks, stable boys, etc."[34] This was a rather insensitive way of saying that gradual emancipation would have caused less immediate disruption of the white society, but one must remember that an evaluation of honest reasoning can be easily distorted by a seemingly accurate quotation. No one knew or could foresee, the consequences of suddenly releasing thousands, later three and one half million, from bondage. Perhaps, he foresaw, and sought to avoid, the disastrous turmoil of the Decade of Reconstruction and the economic and social degradation of the African-Americans in the hundred years that followed.

As for the bondman's viewpoint of gradual emancipation, one can imagine an allied tank approaching a concentration camp. Out steps the tank commander who informs the prisoners that he will liberate a portion of the camp immediately and return for the rest in forty years.

In any event, Lincoln was content that provision had been made for colonization. "I am so far behind the Sumner

---

[33] Lincoln to Congress, April 16, 1862 in [Basler], V, 169.
[34] Segal, 171. Also, Don and Virginia Fehrenbacher, *Recollected Words,* 64.

lighthouse that I will stick to my old colonization hobby," he remarked somewhat ruefully.[35] Lincoln had detected several important defects in the bill, namely, that that there had been no provision made for minors, *femes-covert*[36] (married women), insane or absent owners to present a claim; and that army and navy officers, and others living distant from Washington, could not have presented their claim within the prescribed 90 days specified in the original Act. It is curious that Congress had overlooked these omissions, since there were many capable lawyers in both Houses. Accordingly, Lincoln recommended an amendment or supplemental act. to cure these defects.[37]

Congress remedied these omissions in a supplemental bill, which was signed by the President July 12.[38]

On balance, Lincoln well understood the limitations of District emancipation, which by itself, would do "very little toward getting rid of slavery in the States."[39]

Lincoln had learned many lessons from his experiences with the Delaware and District of Columbia emancipation bills. First, he had found that a small clique of slave owners could easily obstruct progress towards emancipation; and, as a corollary, that the best efforts of Union men were ineffective against this opposition; next, that any realistic sum offered for compensation by the federal government would never satisfy the slave owners; that Slave States would do little to abolish slavery, unless compelled to do so; that gradual emancipation was out of step with the impatient pace of the times; that colonization was completely unacceptable to black society;

---

[35] Fehrenbacher and Fehrenbacher, 295, quotes Lester, 385.
[36] Perhaps Lincoln sought to impress the Congress with this old legal term.
[37] Message to Congress, April 16, 1862.
[38] See Appendix B.
[39] Fehrenbacher and Fehrenbacher, 34; quotes Blodgett, *Autobiography of Henry W. Blodgett*, Waukegan, Ill., 1906.

lastly, that the black community was more concerted and more resolute than he had imagined.

Two great disappointments contributed to Lincoln's growing willingness to modify his hitherto accommodating position on emancipation. First, the inertia of the Army of the Potomac had emboldened the secessionists and had made it increasingly apparent that they would never willingly return to the fold, no matter the inducements. Wrote Henry Halleck, the general-in-chief of the Union Army: "the character the war has very much changed within the last year [1862]. There is now no possible hope of reconciliation...We must conquer the rebels or be conquered by them..."[40]

When the Union army finally did stir, it moved only after preemptory order from Lincoln, and then only as far as Harper's Ferry, thirty-five miles to the west, whereupon it turned back. In March 1862 the army again took to the field, but contrary Lincoln's hopes for a frontal campaign against Richmond, McClelland landed his men on the peninsula between the York and James Rivers and proceeded westward. There, he was bluffed into halting at Yorktown, by a small Confederate force. Despite his abysmal performance, McClelland still found time on July 7, 1862 to warn Lincoln: "A declaration of radical views, especially upon slavery, will rapidly disintegrate our present army."[41]

Another profound disappointment was Lincoln's failure to enlist the support of the Border States for his views on emancipation. While the District of Columbia legislation had been in pendency, Lincoln sent a message to Congress on March 6, 1862, proposing a joint resolution.[42]

---

[40] http://www.ashbrook.org/publicat/oped/owens/07/emancipation.html.
[41] Hessentine, 271.
[42] [Basler], V, 144.

> Resolved that the United States ought to cooperate with
> any state which may adapt gradual abolishment of slavery,
> giving to such state pecuniary aid, to be used by such state
> in its discretion, to compensate for inconveniences public
> and private, produced by such change of system.

Moreover, Lincoln emphasized:

> Such a proposition on the part of the general government
> sets up no claim of a right, by federal authority to interfere
> with slavery within state limits, referring, as it does, the
> absolute control of the subject in each case to the state and
> its people, immediately interested.

With carefully prepared statistics, he demonstrated to the Border States that the slave population in the Border States and in the District of Columbia could be purchased for the amount spent on 87 days of the war. Once again, the cost of emancipation could be paid with 6% bonds. He warned the Border States that "if the war continued long…the institution in your states [slavery] will be extinguished."[43]

Congress had no difficulty passing this resolution. They humored Lincoln, since the probability of implementation was remote. The resolution passed 89-31 in the House, 32-10 in the Senate. Lincoln affixed his signature on April 10th, two days before the District Emancipation Bill emerged from Congress.

The immediate response of the Border States was succinct. "I utterly spit at it and despise it," said Rep. William H. Wadsworth of Kentucky.[44] The other Border State representatives remained steadfast in their opposition, but to many in the North, the proposal had merit. Several northern

---

[43] Medford, 15, in Holzer, Medford and Williams.
[44] Klingaman, 106.

newspapers, including Horace Greeley's New York *Tribune,* greeted the resolution with enthusiasm. Lincoln, who seemed oblivious to the depths of the implacable opposition of the Border States, wrote to Greeley, as if the proposal were still a viable option: "We should urge it [compensated emancipation] "persuasively but not menacingly."[45]

Lincoln allowed the Border States sufficient time to digest his proposal of March 6. Three months later, in the absence of a direct answer, he summoned a delegation of twenty-one Border State Congressmen. After politely listening to his exposition, they enumerated their difficulties with the proposal: emancipation would contravene States Rights; it would disturb the established social order;[46] the amount offered in settlement was insufficient; the country could not afford the cost, etc.. In fact, the war had already drained the United States of its gold and silver, and the California gold supply had long since dried up. As of December 31, 1861, the banks had suspended payment of bank notes in gold and silver.[47]

In short, the delegation rejected Lincoln's proposal by a vote of 20-8.

With its refusal went Lincoln's best efforts to persuade the Slave States to accept a program for the control and management of emancipation. Not willing to altogether abandon hope, he sent another special message to Congress two days after his meeting with the Border States, again proposing compensated emancipation. Congress adjourned without taking action.[48]

---

[45] Lincoln to Greeley, March 24, 1862, in [Basler], V, 162.
[46] Quarles, 107.
[47] Klingaman, 84.
[48] Cox, 9.

LINCOLN SIGNS THE BILL

When Lincoln finally affixed his signature to the District Emancipation Bill, the foreign response was mostly favorable, with some exceptions. From Paris, the journalist wrote that there was much public rejoicing over the Act, but that the enthusiasm was offset by the awful portraits of Lincoln appearing in the shop windows, which reminded the viewer of a recently guillotined murderer.[1] Great Britain seemed less impressed with District Emancipation than with the Union capture of New Orleans.[2] From the West Indies, the Jamaican correspondent reported that "it proved that the nation was becoming Anti-Slavery, and that the doom of the accursed system was only a matter of time."[3] Closer at hand, slave owners in Washington complained of being "plundered of their property" and announced their determination to test the Act before the Supreme Court.[4] Orders were sent to the military commanders to prevent slave owners from forcibly transporting their slaves into Maryland. Some slaves refused to accompany the owners; others, who had been compelled to do so, escaped back to the District.[5]

---

[1] *New York Times,* May 8, 1862, p. 1.
[2] Ford, 146.
[3] *New York Times,* August 21, 1862, p. 6.
[4] Michael Burlingham, [ed]. *Dispatches from Lincoln's White House: The Anonymous Civil War Journalism of Presidential Secretary William O. Stoddard,* 77.
[5] Klingaman, 120.

The abolitionists were jubilant. Writing to Charles Sumner, Frederick Douglass remarked: "the events taking place seem like a dream."[6] Theodore Tilton wrote to Douglass: "The cause is striding forward on seven-league boots." To William Lloyd Garrison, Tilton wrote: "You may see slavery abolished before you have a gray hair on the top of your head."[7] Beecher was wildly enthusiastic: "It is worth living for a lifetime to see the capitol of our government redeemed." George Templeton Strong wrote: "Only the damnedest of 'damned abolitionists' dreamed such a thing a year ago."[8]

Many blacks, some out of loyalty, chose to remain with their owners; others, especially the more elderly, remained in the belief that their white overlords would care for them in their declining years. All but one of the ex-slaves of Francis Blair, Sr. remained with him. His newly freed servant explained, "he [the ex-slave] was used to quality." Another said that he had no thought of leaving but "was delighted that his children are free."[9]

There were many weighty matters which occupied Lincoln's attention during the Spring of 1862. On a personal note, the Lincoln family was recovering from the death of its son, Willie, in February 1862. A desperate depression had overcome Mrs. Lincoln and left her in precarious mental health. The Battle of Shiloh had just been fought on April 6-7, the first of the great Civil War slaughters, leaving an agonizing and unbelievable 23,000 dead or wounded Americans.

---

[6] Foner, *Frederick Douglass,* IV, 233.
[7] McPherson, *Struggle,* 98.
[8] Strong, 216.
[9] Goodwin, 460.

Congress held fast to its colonization *folie*. On May 16, Congress appropriated $500,000 for overseas settlement,[10] in anticipation of the forthcoming Second Confiscation Act, which, for the first time would emancipate the contrabands. As expected, money was offered to aid in their foreign relocation. Lincoln again made reference to colonization in his Annual Message to Congress on December 1, 1862,[11] but by this time it is apparent that the withering opposition from the black community had tempered his enthusiasm:

> Liberia and Hayti are, as yet, the only countries to which colonists of African descent from here could go with certainty of being received and adapted as citizens; *and I regret to say such persons contemplating colonization do not seem so willing to migrate to those countries...*
> [author's italics]

He steadfastly clung to his notions of compensation and colonization, despite the rebuffs. Again, a month before the Emancipation Proclamation was to commence, he proposed a constitutional amendment providing for compensation and voluntary colonization for all States that would abolish slavery before January 1, 1900.

Many in the North credited Seward and Wilson with the District Emancipation initiative, but after Lincoln's resolute refusal on February 4, 1862 to commute the death sentence of the notorious sea slaver, Captain Nathaniel P. Gordon; and with Lincoln's recognition on June 5, 1862 of the Haiti and Liberia governments, together with a cordial reception of the Haitian minister at the White House, Lincoln's anti-slavery credentials were at last validated. As the N.Y. *Times* observed:

---

[10] Lincoln spent only $38,000 of the allotment.
[11] [Basler], Message, December 1, 1862, V, 518.

In his [Lincoln's] pause at this well-marked limit, there may be chagrin for the unconditional Abolitionist; but in his advance so far there is certainly nothing upon which the Pro-Slavery Party, Unionist or Disunionist, can fairly felicitate itself. [12]

The District Emancipation was swiftly followed by other breath-taking, humanitarian initiatives, which had simultaneously been tracking through Congress: April 6, 1862, a more effective treaty with Britain for the suppression of the slave trade;[13] May 1862, a Homestead Act, in which free blacks had not been excluded from government land; June 1862, an act to forever abolish slavery in the territories[14]; July 17, 1862, the Second Confiscation Act, which, as has been shown, conferred freedom on the contrabands.

By this time it was apparent to all that the break with the South was irreconcilable and that there was military merit in the emancipation of slaves held in the states supporting the Confederacy. Many Northerners were waiting impatiently for this, some were angered at the delay, but at least Lincoln had demonstrated his *bona fides*.[15]

Since early summer, Lincoln had been contemplating emancipation by Presidential Decree. The theory advanced was that since the slave was essentially property (Dred Scott), and since property can be confiscated (as with cotton), then slaves too, can be confiscated, and, at the pleasure of the new slave owner (U.S. Government) can be given their freedom. On September 22, following the Battle of Antietam, he published the preliminary draft, but this was merely a non-

---

[12] *New York Times*, August 21, 1862, p. 6.
[13] Henceforth, all slaves taken from captured slavers would be freed.
[14] With no compensation for the slave owners.
[15] *New York Times*, June 24, 1862, p. 4

binding declaration of intent,[16] which still left time for the South to consider halting hostilities. A vain hope. By now, the resolve of the slave squirarchy was unshakable. Despite the Union's staggering defeat at Fredericksburg on December 13th, 1862 with a loss of 12,000 casualties, and against the admonitions of his closest supporters, Lincoln issued the Emancipation Proclamation on January 1, 1863. Even so, he never abandoned his belief in the justice of compensation for the loyal slave holders. As late as one hundred days before the end of the war, he contemplated asking Congress to appropriate 300 million dollars to be apportioned among the slave states, to compensate the slave owner for the loss of his "property."[17]

---

[16] McPherson, *Struggle*, 132.
[17] Lamon, 237.

DISTRICT EMANCIPATION

The President appointed to the District Emancipation Commission, with the approval of the Senate, Daniel R. Goodlow,[1] Horatio King[2] and Samuel Vinton.[3] James G. Barrett[4] was also appointed but refused to serve. Upon the death of Vinton from stroke in June, 1862, John M. Broadhead[5] took his place. Also present at the meetings were Ward Hill Lamon,[6] the Federal Marshal, and William R. Woodward, Clerk.

Notice went out on April 28 that the Commission would be holding sessions at City Hall four days a week and that all loyal owners would have ninety days (until July 11, 1862), to submit in writing a statement of the number, names and ages, description, residence and approximate value of their slaves, for which compensation was sought. The deadline was later extended to August 11. The applicant was required to declare that he was a loyal citizen of the United States, and that he had not brought the slave into the District after April 15; nor had the slave been transferred to him by a rebel. In turn, the commission would determine the value of his holding and report the sum to the Secretary of the Treasury,[7] who would

---

[1] Former Washington correspondent for the *New York Times*.
[2] Postmaster General in the Buchanan administration.
[3] 70 year old Ohio Republican.
[4] Democratic Mayor of Washington.
[5] Maryland Democrat.
[6] Spelled "Lammon" in the commission records.
[7] *New York Times*, May 5, 1862, p. 4.

disperse the monies. Almost three thousand slaves were processed.

For appraising the value of the slave, the members obtained the services of B.M. Campbell, an experienced slave dealer, formerly from New Orleans.[8] He began by noting that slave values had fallen with the influx of contrabands.[9] The commission chose a somewhat circuitous method of calculation. After lengthy deliberation, it decided to accept $2,074,000 as the value of the slaves prior to the conflict. Since Congress had appropriated one million dollars, the commission established an approximate reimbursement rate of 48.3%.[10]

The commission got off to a slow start. From April 16-28, only 50 bondmen had been processed.[11]

The work was often contentious and required careful judgment. One example was the determination of value for a slave, held for the duration of the life of his owner. The commission was required to assess value, based on the owner's life expectancy. Another example was the determination of value for a slave held in bondage until the payment of specified sum.

Other similar difficulties tested the ingenuity of the commission:[12]

> **Number 689.** A slave belonging to a rebel sympathizer who had been given to a Union man in payment of a promissory note. (claim accepted)

---

[8] Quarles, 106.
[9] Clark-Lewis, 12.
[10] Johnston, 175.
[11] *New York Times*, May 5, 1862, p. 4.
[12] National Archives Microfilm Publication 520, roll 1. Records of Commissioners for the Emancipation of Slavery in the District of Columbia, 1862-63.

Number 912. Slave children currently owned by the wife of a man who defected to Richmond before the children were born. (rejected)

Number 589. A District resident who owns eight slaves was a former resident of Fairfax County, Virginia and voted for the Ordinance of Secession.(rejected)

Number 535. A owner with no clear title to three slaves. (rejected)

Number 666. Nine slaves for whom no application was made. (claim abandoned)

Number 661. Claimant unable to produce the slave, who fled the District. (claim accepted)

Many slaves had fled the District before April 16, and upon receiving supporting proof, the commission accepted the claims of their owners.

Of the 909 applications, 36 were rejected wholly and 21 in part.[13] The commission paid an average of $400 for each of the 2,989 slaves, totaling $903,406. The highest claim made was for three slaves, each valued at $2,000. The value of Philip Reid, who helped cast the statue of Freedom (soon to be erected atop the dome of the Capitol) was set at $ 350.[14] The largest slave holding was 68. In many instances, reimbursement was much less than what the bondman would have fetched at auction. A black laborer could have brought as much as $1,400 in open market. Some owners were paid only a token sum, merely to satisfy an appearance of "compensation." A few slave owners declined to receive

---

[13] Clark-Lewis, 60
[14] http://uschscapitolhistory.usch.org.

payment, "but were thankful to have the United States Government take charge of old and decrepit slaves that they have been supplying" These unfortunates could now be thrown onto the street. One hundred owners refused to take an oath of allegiance[15] and did not file a claim. Nine of the slave owners were African-American. Some of them might have "owned" kin, whom they kept under "protective custody," since in times gone by, there were numerous obstacles to setting them free.[16]

On July 16 the commission published a list of the slave owners in the newspapers and requested that anyone with knowledge of bogus claims make known that information.

While the commission was still in session, Congress passed the Supplemental Act on July 12. This allowed claims to be presented by persons who, for one reason or another, had not previously applied; and also by black bondmen whose owners had not made claim. The commission received an additional 161 claims and accepted 139. By August 16, 1862, having completed its work,[17] the commission adjourned; but continued to hold irregular meeting until January 14, 1863.

The black population of the District, free and enslaved, sensed what few of white society could comprehend. What their lives had lacked, for the most part, was not so much food nor shelter, but the dignity that freedom alone could bestow-- the right to choose, to work for themselves, to pick up and go, to raise their families without fear of separation, to learn to read and write, to do all the innumerable things that freemen take for granted.

---

[15] Johnston, 175.

[16] Virginia, for example, forbade the newly emancipated to reside in the state after six months [Lewis, 22].

[17] Milburn, 118.

To be sure, with freedom come hardships. Some of the newly-freed had lost their employment and their dwelling. Some had to labor for low wages.[18] The chasm between freedman and freeman was still enormous. But they were free!

Signs of improvement in the black community were immediate. After the passage of a Senate resolution spurning color disqualifications for United States mail carriers,[19] the Postmaster General issued instructions that all black postmen were to have equal rights. Burdensome restrictions on the black entrepreneur were lifted. Now, black people could attend the theater, since they were no longer bound by a ten o'clock curfew.[20] They continued to be seated in the worst seats in the building.

Before the emancipation, Washington had had fifteen academies for black students,[21] offering education for one thousand black children,[22] mostly the offspring of freedmen. The remaining 2,175, mostly slave children, went without education. Now, schooling was provided for all black children in the District, who hitherto had been excluded from the public schools, despite the property taxes paid by their parents, for the support of the schools from which their children had been barred.

On April 29, 1862 Grimes (Rep.) of Iowa introduced a school bill providing for the education of black children in the District. A similar bill was introduced in the Senate on May 8. The bill enjoined the municipal authorities of Washington and Georgetown to set aside 10% of the money received from taxes on real estate and personal property belonging to "people

---

[18] Clark-Lewis, 10.
[19] Ibid., 77.
[20] Green, *Secret City*, 60.
[21] Lewis, 44.
[22] Green, *Washington,* I, 185.

of color," to be spent on primary schools for the education of black children, under the direction of a separate board of trustees appointed by the Secretary of the Interior.[23] The bill passed both houses and was signed by the President on May 21, 1862.[24]

The Black Codes were repealed. No longer were freedmen required to post a bond in order to remain in the city. African-Americans could now testify in court. If tried in the District, he would have the same right as the white man, but could not serve on juries nor vote. As one author sagely noted, "They were clearly second class citizens, but at least they were citizens."[25]

Street omnibuses were made accessible for the first time to black and white alike. No longer was the African American required to wait for a special black omnibus, which ran less frequently. This change came about after a black surgeon, Major A.T. Augusta, was excluded from an omnibus while on route for court martial duty. He was compelled to walk to his destination in a storm. [26]

If the lot of the black people in Washington did not improve in all respects as completely or as quickly as some had wished, at least there was optimism for the future. But many of the newly freed remained in great need, and public assistance was scarce. As Elizabeth Keckley observed: "Instead of flowery path, days of perpetual sunshine…the sunshine was eclipsed by shadows and the mute appeals for help—to often were answered by cold neglect."[27] Fortunately, the military was able to employ increasingly large numbers of

---

[23] Green, *Washington,* I, 280.
[24] Wilson, 184-193.
[25] Finkelman, III, 268. [The Fourteenth Amendment granted citizenship in 1868.]
[26] Brooks, 193.
[27] Keckley, 112.

the new freedmen as laborers, and after September 1863, enlistments in the United States Colored Regiments were begun.

To the black population of the District, the passage of the District Emancipation Act was an occasion for ecstatic jubilation. Better than many whites around them, they sensed that a new era was dawning, that the scourge of bondage was nearing its end and that deliverance for their enslaved brethren would surely follow. On Sunday, April 20, every black church in the District held special service of prayer and thanksgiving, "with singing, shouting, praying, weeping or jumping, all without direction from the pulpit"[28] The Fifteen Street Colored Presbyterian Church congregation expressed their thanks to God and assured the public that it would prove worthy of its confidence.[29] The black community in New York held its celebration on May 5.[30] Festivities took the form of a gigantic fair, held in East New York. Alas, the celebration was interrupted by a torrential rain storm.[31]

Not until the war's end was a grand celebration held in the District. On April 16, 1866, a year after the war had ended, the fourth anniversary of the District Emancipation was commemorated. Among its organizers was Elizabeth Keckley, a seamstress-confident and loyal friend of Mary Todd Lincoln and a member of the important First Colored Presbyterian Church. African-American children were excused from school attendance for the day. All of Washington's black political, social and athletic clubs participated in the festivities.

Five thousand marchers, including two regiments of U.S. Colored Troops, resplendent in their blue uniforms, assembled

---

[28] Quarles, 105.
[29] Clark-Lewis, 78.
[30] Quarles, 105.
[31] *New York Times*, August 5, 1862, p. 2.

on the White House grounds. Cannons boomed, and the bands played martial airs.

President Andrew Johnson met the marchers and was greeted with three loud cheers. After thanking the crowd, he began by cautioning them not to trust those [Radical Republicans] who had chosen them "as a hobby and pretence." He told them that he had contributed more than any man in procuring the Thirteenth Amendment, forever ending slavery in the United States. He did this, he said, not to gain power but to establish freedom in a cause which he had periled his all.[32]

The President concluded, "Let me mingle with you in celebration of the day, which commenced your freedom." He descended the steps and shook hands with his audience. The marchers then reformed and paraded along Pennsylvania Avenue to the Capitol. Cheer after cheer were given the Congressmen. Ten thousand spectators were on hand to applaud enthusiastically.

The marchers then paraded to Franklin Square, where thousands of spectators had assembled around a platform decorated with flags on both sides and draped in festoons on the facade corners. In front of the stand was a message from Lincoln:

> Fellow-citizens of the Senate and House of
> Representatives. This act entitled 'an act for the
> release of certain persons held to service in the
> District of Columbia' has been approved and signed.
>
> April 16, 1862 A. Lincoln

---

[32] Johnson compelled the southern states to accept the Thirteenth Amendment as a condition for reentering the Union.

Figure 4. Emancipation Day Celebration in the District 1866. From *Harper's Weekly*, May 12, 1866.

On the top of the platform read the inscription:

> Lincoln, the Liberator of millions; his great work is done, and he sleeps in peace in the great praise of the West. We are loyal to God and our country. This is the Lord's doing and it is marvelous in our eyes.

Also:

> We have received our civil right. Give us the right of suffrage and the work is done. [The Fifteenth Amendment granting male suffrage was passed in 1870.]

Speakers of the day included Rev. Henry Highland Garnett,[33] Senator Lyman Trumbull[34] and Hon. Henry Wilson,[35] the venerable abolitionist, who had introduced the District Emancipation Bill in the Senate.

Washington's black elite continued to organize and direct the celebrations, served as marshals and selected the speakers. Fredrick Douglass, later a U.S. Marshal and a resident of Washington, was a frequent guest.

As the years passed, some spectators became somewhat disorderly, and the black elite promptly withdrew their support for the parade, as did Frederick Douglass.[36] Two parades were hastily organized to replace the grand parade, but President Grover Cleveland refused to review either. After 1901, the parade petered out, although it continued to be celebrated in several churches. Many worshipers still recalled with awe and

---

[33] First African-American to address Congress.
[34] Introduced the Thirteenth Amendment Bill into the Senate.
[35] *Harper's Weekly*, May 12, 1866.
[36] Clark-Lewis, 130.

reverence the tumultuous scene of that fateful day on April 16, 1862.

In 2002, as a result of research and lobbying done by Ms. Loretta Carter-Hanes, the holiday was revived. Three years later, the day was made a public holiday and spirited efforts now are being made to insure that the day is never forgotten.[37]

---

[37] Elsewhere, emancipation is celebrated in Florida (May 20), Puerto Rico (March 22), Texas (June 19). In the Caribbean, the celebrations are held during the first week in August, since slavery was abolished in the British Empire on August 22, 1834.

S. 108.

IN THE HOUSE OF REPRESENTATIVES.

APRIL 9, 1862.

Read a first and second time, committed to the Committee of the Whole House on the state of the Union, and ordered to be printed.

AN ACT

For the release of certain persons held to service or labor in the District of Columbia.

1   *Be it enacted by the Senate and House of Representa-*

2   *tives of the United States of America in Congress assembled,*

3   That all persons held to service or labor within the District of

4   Columbia, by reason of African descent, are hereby discharged

5   and freed of and from all claim to such service or labor; and

6   from and after the passage of this act neither slavery nor in-

7   voluntary servitude, except for crime, whereof the party shall

8   be duly convicted, shall hereafter exist in said District.

1   SEC. 2. *And be it further enacted,* That all persons loyal

2   to the United States holding claims to service or labor against

3   persons discharged therefrom by this act may, within ninety

4   days from the passage thereof, but not thereafter, present to

5   the commissioners hereinafter mentioned their respective

6   statements or petitions in writing, verified by oath or affirma-

7   tion, setting forth the names, ages, and personal description

Figure 5. Face piece of The District Emancipation Act.

APPENDIX A

An Act for the Release of certain Persons held to Service or Labor in the District of Columbia.

Be it enacted by the Senate and House of Representatives of the United States of America in Congress assembled, That all persons held to service or labor within the District of Columbia by reason of African descent are hereby discharged and freed of and from all claim to such service or labor, and from and after the passage of this act neither slavery nor involuntary servitude, except for crime, whereof the party shall be duly convicted, shall hereafter exist in said District.

SEC. 2. *And be it further enacted,* That all persons loyal to the United States, holding claims to service or labor against persons discharged there from by this act, may, within ninety days from the passage thereof, but not thereafter, present to the commissioners hereinafter mentioned their respective statements or petitions in writing, verified by oath or affirmation, setting forth the names, ages, and personal description of such persons, the manner in which said petitioners acquired such claim, and any facts touching the value thereof, and declaring his allegiance to the Government of the United States, and that he has not borne arms against the United States during the present rebellion; nor in any way given aid or comfort thereto: *Provided,* That the oath of the party to the petition shall not be evidence of the facts therein stated.

SEC. 3. *And be it further enacted,* That the President of the United States, with the advice and consent of the Senate, shall appoint three commissioners, residents of the District of Columbia, any two of whom shall have power to act, who shall receive the petitions above mentioned, and who shall

investigate and determine the validity and value of the claims
therein presented, as aforesaid, and appraise and apportion,
under the proviso hereto annexed, the value in money of the
several claims by them found to be valid:
Provided, however, That the entire sum so appraised and
apportioned shall not excee in the aggregate an amount equal
to three hundred dollars for each person shown to have been
so held by lawful claim: *And provided further:* That no claim
shall be allowed for any slave or slaves brought into said
District after the passage of this act, nor for any slave claimed
by any person who has borne arms against the Government of
the United States in the present rebellion, or in any way given
aid or comfort thereto, or which originates in or by virtue of
any transfer heretofore made, or which shall hereafter be made
by any person who has in any manner aided or sustained the
rebellion against the Government of the United States.

SEC. 4. *And be it further enacted,* That said commissioners
shall, within nine months from the passage of this act, make a
full and final report of their proceedings, findings, and
appraisement, and shall deliver the same to the Secretary of
the Treasury, which report shall be deemed and taken to be
conclusive in all respects, except as hereinafter provided; and
the Secretary of the Treasury shall, with like excerption, cause
the amounts so apportioned to said claims to be paid from the
Treasury of the United States to the partie4s found by said
report to be entitled thereto as aforesaid, and the same shall be
received in full and complete compensation: *Provided,* That in
cases where petitions may be filed presenting conflicting
claims, or setting up liens, said commissioners shall so specify
in said report, and payment shall not be made according to the
award of said commissioners until a period of sixty days shall
have elapsed, during which time any petitioner claiming an
interest in the particular amount may file a bill in equity in the
Circuit Court of the District of Columbia, making all other
claimants defendants thereto, setting forth the proceedings in

such case before said commissioners and their action therein, and praying that the party to whom payment has been awarded may be en-joined from receiving the same; and if said court shall grant such pro-visional order, a cop thereof may, on motion of said complainant, be served upon the Secretary of the treasury, who shall thereupon cause the said amount of money to be paid into said court, subject to its orders and final decree, which payment shall be in full and complete compensation, as in other cases.

SEC. 5. *And be it further enacted,* That said commissioners shall hold their sessions in the city of Washington, at such place and times as the President of the United States may direct, of which they shall give due and public notice. They shall have power to subpoena and compel the attendance of witnesses, and to receive testimony and enforce its production, as in civil cases before courts of justice, without the exclusion of any witness on account of color; and they may summon before them the persons making claim to service or labor, and examine them under oath; and they may also, for the purposes of identification and appraisement, call before them the persons so claimed. Said commissioners shall appoint a clerk, administer oaths and affirmations in said proceedings, and who shall issue all lawful process by them ordered. The Marshal of the district of Columbia shall personally, or by deputy, attend upon the sessions of said commissioners, and shall execute the process issued by said clerk.

SEC. 6. *And be it further enacted,* That said commissioners shall receive in compensation for their services the sum of two thousand dollars each, to be paid upon the filing of their report; that said clerk shall receive for his services the sum of two hundred dollars per month; that said marshal shall receive such fees as are allowed by law for similar services performed by him in the Circuit Court of the District of Columbia; that the Secretary of the treasury shall cause all other reasonable expenses of said commission to be audited and allowed, and that said compensation, fees, and expenses shall be paid from the Treasury of the United States.

SEC. 7. *And be it further enacted,* That for the purpose of carrying this act into effect there is hereby appropriated, out of any money in the treasury not otherwise appropriated, a sum not exceeding one millions of dollars.

SEC. 8. *And be it further enacted.* That an person or persons who shall kidnap, or in any manner transport or procure to be taken out of said District, any person or persons discharged and freed by the provisions of this act, or any free person or persons with intent to re-enslave or sell such person or persons into slavery, or shall re-enslave any of said freed persons, the person or persons so offending shall be deemed guilty of a felony, and on conviction thereof in any court of competent jurisdiction in said District, shall be imprisoned in the penitentiary not less than five nor more than twenty years.

SEC. 9. *And be it further enacted,* That within twenty days, or within such further time as the commissioners herein provided for shall limit, after the passage of this act, a statement in writing or schedule shall be filed with the clerk of the circuit Court for the District of Columbia, by the several owners or claimants to the services of the persons made free or manumitted by this act, setting forth the names, ages, sex, and particular description of such persons, severally; and the said clerk shall receive and record, in a book by him to be provided and kept for that purpose, the said statements or schedules on receiving fifty cents each therefore, and no claim shall be allowed to any claimant or owner who shall neglect this requirement..

SEC. 10. *And be it further enacted,* That the said clerk and his successors in office shall, from time to time, on demand, and on receiving twenty-five cents therefore, prepare, sign, and deliver to each person made free or manumitted by this act, a certificate under the seal of said court, setting out the name, age, and description of such person, and stating that such person was duly manumitted and set free by this act.

SEC. 11. *And be it further enacted.* That the sum of one hundred thousand dollars, out of any money in the Treasury not otherwise appropriated, is hereby appropriated, to be expended under the direction of the President of the United States, to aid in the colonization and settlement of such free persons of African descent now residing in said District, including those to be liberated by this act, as may desire to emigrate to the republics of Hayti or Liberia, or such other country beyond the limits of the United States as the President ma determine: *Provided,* The expenditure for this purpose shall not exceed one hundreds dollars for each emigrant.

SEC. 12. *And be it further enacted,* That all acts of Congress and all laws of the State of Maryland in force in said district, and all ordinances of the cities of Washington and Georgetown, inconsistent with the pro-visions of this act, are hereby repealed.

APPROVED, April 16, 1862.

APPENDIX B

An Act supplementary to the "Act for the Release of Certain Persons held to Service or Labor in the District of Columbia," approved April sixteen, eighteen hundred and sixty-two.

Be it enacted by the Senate and House of Representatives of the United States of America in Congress assembled, That the oath or affirmation required by the second section of the act entitled "An act for the release of certain persons held to service or labor in the District of Columbia," to verify the statements or petitions in writing filed before the commissioners, under the act aforesaid, Of persons holding claim to service or labor against persons of African descent, freed and discharged therefrom, under the act aforesaid, may in all cases in which the persons holding claims, as aforesaid, are infants or minors, be made by the guardian or by any other person, whether separately or jointly, having the custody, management, or control by law of the person and property of such infants or minors; and that in all cases in which the persons holding claims as aforesaid are non-residents of the District of Columbia, or resident absentees, the oath or affirmation required as aforesaid may be made by the attorney or agent of said non-resident or resident absentees; and in all cases in which the statements or petitions, required as aforesaid, of persons in the military or naval service of the United States, shall have been or may be hereafter verified before any commander of any military post, or of any officer having a separate command of any military force in the field, or before any captain, commander, or lieutenant commanding in the navy, the same as if the verification had bee nor were made before any officer competent by law to take and administer oaths and affirmations: *Provided,* That the commissioners shall be satisfied that, at the time of the verification aforesaid, the person making the same was employed in the military or naval service of the United States within the jurisdiction of a rebellious State or Territory, and unable to make the oath or affirmation required, as aforesaid, before any officer authorized by law to take or administer the same, holding allegiance to the United States.

SEC. 2. *And be it further enacted,* That if any person having claim to the service or labor of any person or persons in the District of Columbia by reason of African descent, shall neglect or refuse to file with the clerk of the circuit court of the District of Columbia the statement in writing or schedule provided in the ninth section of the act approved April sixteen, eighteen hundred and sixty-two, to which this is supplementary, then it shall be lawful for the person or persons, whose services are claimed as aforesaid, to file such statement in writing or schedule setting forth the particular facts mentioned in said ninth section; and the said clerk shall receive and record the same as provided in said section, on receiving fifty cents each therefore.

SEC. 3.*And be it further enacted,* That whenever the facts set forth in the said statement or schedule shall be found by the commissioners to be true, the said clerk and his successors in office shall prepare, sign, and deliver certificates, as prescribed in the tenth section of the act to which this is supplementary, to such person or persons as shall file their statements in pursuance of the foregoing section, in all respect the same as if such statements were filed by the person having claim to their service or labor.

SEC. 4. *And be it further enacted,* That all persons held to service or labor under the laws of any State, and who at any time since the sixteenth day of April, anno Domini eighteen hundred and sixty-two, by the consent of the person to whom such service or labor is claimed to be owing, have been actually employed within the District of Columbia, or shall be hereafter thus employed, are hereby declared free, and forever released from such servitude, anything in the laws of the United States or of any State to the contrary notwithstanding.

SEC. 5. *And be it further enacted,* That in all judicial proceedings in the District of Columbia there shall be no exclusion of any witness on account of color.

APPROVED, July 12, 1862.

BIBLIOGRAPHY

Appish, Kwame Anthony, and Gates, Henry Louis. *Africa*. 5 vols. NY: Oxford, 2005.

Belz, Herman. *Abraham Lincoln Constitutionalism and Equal Rights in the Civil War Era*. NY: Fordham, 1998.

Bennett, Lerone. *Forced into Glory*. Chicago: Johnson, 2000.

Basler, Roy P. and Chrisian O. Basler. *The Collected Works of Abraham Lincoln*. 9 vols. New Brunswick: Rutgers University Press, 1953.

Berlin, Ira, ed. *Free at Last*. NY: New Press, 1992.

Beveredge, Albert J. *Abraham Lincoln 1809-1858*. 2 vols. Boston: Houghton-Mifflin, 1928.

Bowers, Claude F. *The Tragic Era*. Cambridge: Houghton Mifflin, 1929.

Brooks, Noah. *Washington in Lincoln's Times*. Chicago: Quadrangle, 1971. (Reprint of Chicago: Century, 1895 edition.)

Browning, Theodore Calvin Pease, and James G. Randall, eds. *The Diary of Orville Hickman Browning*. 2 vols. Springfield: Illinois State Historical Society, 1925.

Burchard, Peter. *Lincoln and Slavery*. NY: Athenaeum, 1999.

Carwardine, Richard. *Lincoln*. NY: Knopf, 2006.

Clark-Lewis, Elizabeth, ed. *First Freed*. Washington, DC: Howard University Press, 2002.

Clephane, Walter. "The Local Aspect of Slavery in the District of Columbia." *Records of the Columbia Historical Society*, Vol. 3, March 6, 1899, Washington: Published by the Society, 1900.

Cox, La Wanda. *Lincoln and Black Freedom*. Urbana: University of Illinois, 1985.

De la Escosura, Leandro Prados, ed. *Exceptionalism and Industrialization*. Cambridge: Cambridge University, 2004.

Dickens, Charles. *American Notes and Picture of Italy.* NY: Oxford, 1987.

Donald, David. *Charles Sumner and the Rights of Man.* NY: Knopf, 1970.

Douglas, William O. *Lincoln and the Negroes.* NY: Atheneum, 1963.

DuBois, W. E. B. *Black Reconstruction in America, 1860-1880.* NY: Harcourt Brace, 1935.

Fehrenbacher, Don E. and Virginia Fehrenbacher. *Recollected Words.* Stanford: Stanford University Press, 1996.

Finkelman, Paul, ed. *Encyclopedia of African American History, 1619-1895.* 3 vols. NY: Oxford, 2006.

Fish, Carl Russell. *The Rise of the Common Man.* NY: Macmillan, 1967.

Fleischner, Jennifer. *Mrs. Lincoln and Mrs. Keckley.* NY:Broadway, 2003.

Foner, Philip S. *Life and Writings of Frederick Douglass.* 5 vols. NY: International, 1952.

Foner, Eric, ed. *Our Lincoln.* NY: Norton, 2008.

Ford, Worthington C. *A Cycle of Adams Letters.* Boston: Houghton Mifflin, 1920.

Freidel, Frank, ed. *Union Pamphlets of the Civil War, 1861-65.* Cambridge: Harvard, 1967.

Goodwin, Doris Kearns. *Team of Rivals.* NY: Simon and Schuster, 2005.

Green, Constance M. *Washington, Village and Capitol, 1800-1876.* 2 vols. Princeton: Princeton, 1962.

Green, Constance M. *The Secret City.* Princeton: Princeton, 1969.

Green, Constance M. *A History of the Capitol, 1800-1950.* Princeton: Princeton, 1976.

Grund, Frances. *Aristocracy in America.* Gloucester, MA: Smith, 1968. (Reprint of 1839 edition.)

Guelzo, Allen. *Lincoln's Emancipation Proclamation.* NY: Simon and Schuster, 2005.

Hall, Basil. *Travels in North America.* Philadelphia: Carey, Lee and Carey, 1829.

Hamilton, Thomas. *Men and Manners in America.* Edinburgh: Blackwood, 1843.

Heidler, David S. and Jeanne T. Heidler. *Encyhclopedia of the American Civil War.* 5 vols. Santa Barbara, CA: ABC-Clio, 2000.

Hesseltine, William B. *The Tragic Conflict.* NY: Braziller, 1962.

Holzer, Harold, Edna Medford, and Frank T. Williams. *The Emancipation Proclamation.* Baton Rouge, LA: Louisiana State, c. 2006.

Johnston, Allen. *Surviving Freedom.* NY: Garland, 1993.

Keckley, Elizabeth. *Behind the Scenes.* NY: Oxford, 1988.

Klingaman, William K. *Abraham Lincoln and the Road to Emancipation.* NY: Viking, 2001.

Lamon, Ward Hill (Dorothy Lamon Teillard, ed.). *Recollections of Abraham Lincoln.* Lincoln: University Nebraska, 1994. (Reprint of Mclure, 1911 edition.)

Lester, Charles Edwards. *Life and Public Services of Charles Sumner.* NY: U.S. Publ. Co, 1874.

Lewis, David. *District of Columbia.* NY: Norton, 1976.

Mackay, Alex. *The Western World.* NY: Negro University Press, 1966. (Reprint of 1846 edition.)

McPherson, James M. *The Struggle for Equality.* Princeton: Princeton, 1964.

Milburn, Page. *The Emancipation of Slaves.* Records of the Columbia Historical Soc., 1912. Read before the Society April 16, 1912.

Miller, William Lee. *Arguing about Slavery.* NY: Knopf, 1996.

Neely, Mark E. *The Abraham Lincoln Encyclopedia.* NY: McGraw-Hill, 1982.

Nicolay, John G. and John Hay. *Abraham Lincoln A History.* 10 vols. NY: Century, 1917.

Quarles, Benjamin. *Lincoln and the Negro.* NY: Oxford, 1962.

Ransom, Roger L. *Economics of Civil War.* http://eh.net/encyclopedia/article/ransom.civilwar.us

Russell, William Howard. *My Diary North and South.* Gloucester, MA: Smith, 1969.

Sandburg, Carl. *Abraham Lincoln: The War Years.* 4 vols. Harcourt, Brace, 1937.

Segal, Charles M. *Conversations with Lincoln.* NY: Putnam, 1961.

Staudenraus, P.J. *The African Colonization Movement, 1816-1865.* NY: Columbia Univ. Press, 1961.

Stern, Philip van Doren. *The Life and Writings of Abraham Lincoln.* NY: Random House, 1940.

Strong, George Templeton. (ed. Allan Nevins). *Diary of the Civil War.* NY: Macmillan, 1962.

Thomas, Benjamin and Hyman, Harold M. *Stanton.* NY: Knopf, 1962.

Trollope, Anthony. *North America.* NY: Knopf, 1951.

Wilson, Henry. *History of the Antislavery Measures.* NY: Negro University Press, 1969. (Reprint of 1864 edition.)

INDEX

A

Abolition
France, 17
Great Britain and West Indies, 17
Abolition literature, severe punishment for possession, 8
Abolitionists
petition in DC, 12
wanted a bolder approach to emancipation, 32
Adams, John Quincy, objected to abolition in DC, 12
African-Americans, laborers in Washington, 5
Alexander II, Czar of Russia, abolition of slavery, 24
Alexandria, Virginia
contrabands, 26
retroceded, 2
Anacostia River, 1
Antietam, Battle of, 66
Apprenticeship, explanation, 26
Army of the Potomac, inertia, 59
Ashley, Rep. (OH), 44, 48
Augusta, Maj. A. T., black surgeon, 74

B

Barrett, James G., 69
Bayard, Dem. (DE), 41
Beecher, Henry Ward, 51, 64
Benefits, for relocated liberated slaves, 46
Bill #S108, Emancipation in DC, 43, 44, 45, 46
passed in House of Representatives, 46
Bingham (OH), 44

Black Codes, 7, 8
repealed after emancipation, 74
Blair, Francis Sr., 64
Blair, Rep. (MO), 43
Blake, Rep. (OH), 44
"Blue Jug" (Washington prison), 29, 30
Boone, Daniel, 14
Breckenridge, John C., 1860
Southern Democrat presidential candidate, 25
British Guinea, considered for colonization, 52
British Honduras, considered for colonization, 52
Broadhead, John M., 69
Browning, 41
Browning, Sen. Orville H., 50
Buchanan, President, objected to abolition in DC, 12
Bull Run, First Battle of, 27
Butler, Gen Benjamin F., 27

C

Calvert, Opp. (MD), 48
Campbell, J. M., slave dealer/appraiser, 70
Capitol building, built with slave labor, 2
Capitol grounds, nearness to columns of chained slaves, 8
Caribbean Islands, agricultural decline after compensated emancipation, 18
Carlson, Roxanne, viii
Carter-Hanes, Loretta, 79
Civil War, 64
Clark, Rep. (NH), 41
Clay, Henry, 12, 52

ABOUT THE AUTHOR

Dr. J. C. Ladenheim, a retired neurosurgeon, has been a lifelong student of nineteenth-century American history and a past president of the Abraham Lincoln Association of Jersey City, the oldest Lincoln association in the United States.

.

www.ingramcontent.com/pod-product-compliance
Lightning Source LLC
Chambersburg PA
CBHW052131090426
42741CB00009B/2033